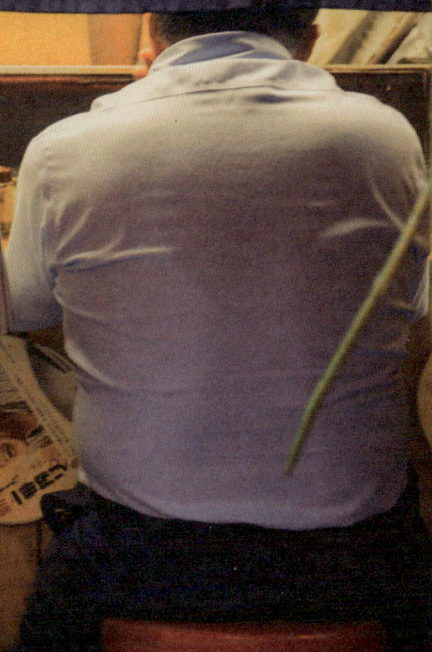

DELICIOUS JAPANESE STREET EATS

LAURE KIÉ

鳥 やきとり

やきとり

やきとり

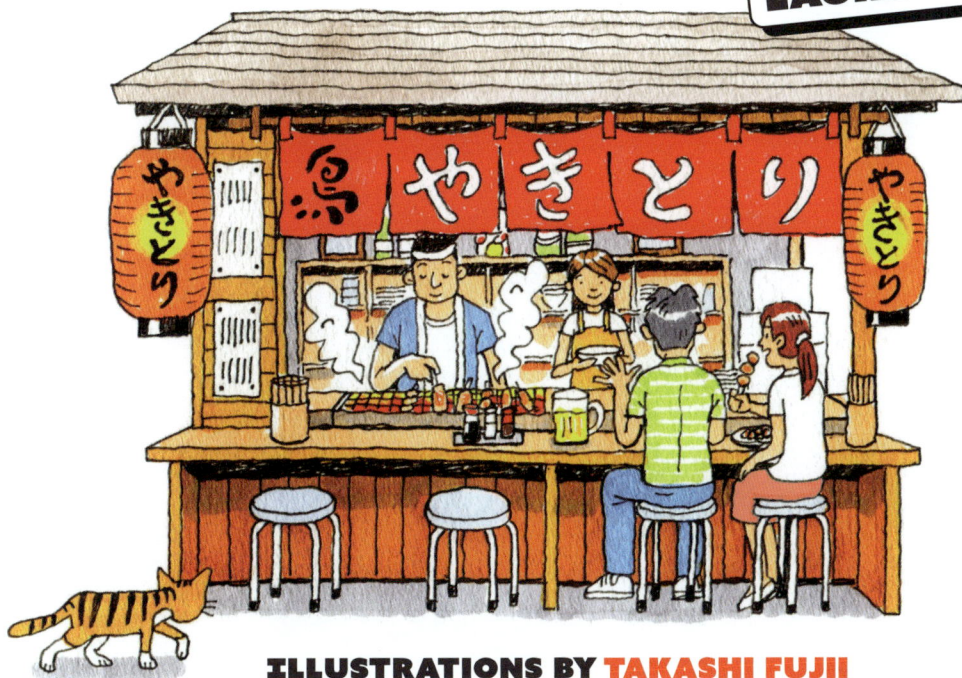

ILLUSTRATIONS BY TAKASHI FUJII

TUTTLE Publishing

Tokyo | Rutland, Vermont | Singapore

CONTENTS

Street Treats

Japan, renowned for its refined cuisine, is also a great street food destination. Whether it's during matsuri (festivals) or in designated areas of the nation's major cities, rows of street stalls, called yataï, offer a variety of popular dishes: takoyaki, ramen, okonomiyaki, taiyaki, yakitori, onigiri and so many more. So many tempting offerings! The dishes on display are rich and varied, sending you on a deliciously memorable tasting tour while discovering an important part of Japanese gastronomic culture.

Itadakimasu* !

*Bon appétit !

WELCOME TO THE AMAZING WORLD OF JAPANESE STREET EATS!

In Japan, as in the rest of Asia, there's a strong street food culture, where it's common to eat on the go—whether while waiting for a train on the platform or during traditional festivals on temple grounds. This type of cuisine is ubiquitous and highly diverse, reflecting Japan's geography, and the variety of homegrown ingredients the nation produces.

Tonkotsu ramen p. 62

FUKUOKA

KYUSHU

•Naha

OKINAWA

Yaki-imo p. 34

Miso ramen p. 54

HOKKAIDO

Sapporo

Kaisendon p. 138

Miyagi

Niigata

Kushikatsu p. 114

HONSHU

Tokyo

Okonomiyaki p. 46

Matcha p. 196

Kyoto

Nagoya

Hiroshima

Okayama

Osaka

Tsukiji p. 128

SHIKOKU

Takoyaki p. 43

THE MUST-HAVES AND THE MUST-TRIES

Japanese street stalls offer a range of sweet and salty snacks and specialties. Here are 12 key offerings you won't want to miss!

ラーメン
1. RAMEN

These wheat noodles originated in China and were introduced to Japan in the early 20th century, where they were served in soy sauce or miso-based broths. There's nothing like a steaming bowl of ramen at a yataï counter (p. 54)!

たこ焼き
2. TAKOYAKI

Takoyaki, meaning "grilled octopus," are small grilled dumplings stuffed with the tentacled treat. This Osaka specialty has become the symbol of Japanese street food (p. 43).

焼き鳥
3. YAKITORI

Yakitori translates as "grilled chicken." They're tasty little skewers cooked on the barbecue and dipped in a sauce called, naturally, yakitori sauce (p. 24).

焼きそば
4. YAKISOBA

These pan-fried noodles are a street food staple. They're most often sautéed with vegetables and meat, then coated in a thick, slightly sweet sauce (p. 44).

おにぎり
5. ONIGIRI

The Japanese enjoy these versatile snacks any time of day. These easily portable rice packets are mainly sold in konbini and railway stations (p. 120).

お好み焼き
6. OKONOMIYAKI

There's a variation served in Hiroshima that includes noodles (p. 46), but the Osaka original is a street-fare classic!

コロッケ
7. KOROKKE

Korokke are delicious croquettes, usually made from potato and meat, breaded with panko breadcrumbs to give them an incomparable crunch (p. 100).

カレーパン
8. CURRY PAN

These curry-filled buns are the perfect example of the Westernization of Japanese cuisine. Soft on the inside, crispy on the outside, curry pan (or karepan) has become a popular snack enjoyed throughout the day (p. 158).

串揚げ
9. KUSHIAGE

These breaded skewers called both kushikatsu and kushiage are a specialty of Osaka. A wide variety of ingredients can be found on these skewers: beef, pork, shrimp or vegetables (p. 114).

鯛焼き
10. TAÏYAKI

These fish-shaped cakes filled with anko red bean paste or cream custard are often prepared in street stalls. In Japan, fish are thought to bring good forutne and these cakes are often served for celebrations (p. 182).

団子
11. DANGO

These savory or sweet treats are small mochi dumplings (made from glutinous rice paste) presented on skewers. They're a common sight at festivals, sometimes tinted green and pink to make them more festive (p. 162).

かき氷
12. KAKIGORI

Crushed ice topped with colored syrup, this guilty pleasure is a great answer to the hot, humid Japanese summers. Numerous stands at festivals and near temples offer these refreshing shaved ice cups in a wide range of flavors (p. 174).

WHERE CAN I EAT THE BEST STREET FOOD?

Street food is ubiquitous in Japan, but strangely enough, it's forbidden to nibble while walking in the street, except during matsuri (festivals) or in designated areas at food markets.

屋台

YATAÏ STREET STALLS

These gathering spots, which developed in the aftermath of World War II, offer simple cuisine in a friendly atmosphere. Today, they've become synonymous with Japanese street food (p. 12).

祭り

MATSURI FESTIVALS

Often linked to Shinto celebrations and taking place on the outskirts of temples, these popular festivals are the ideal time to sample street food. Yakisoba, takoyaki, taiyaki and kakigori are just some of the treats on offer.

市場

MARKETS

These are typically permanent establishments, the best known of which are Amyoko and Tsukiji in Tokyo, Nishiki in Kyoto and Kuromon in Osaka. These spots are ideal for sampling a whole range of popular Japanese cuisine.

Ameyoko Market

横丁

YOKOCHO FOOD ALLEYS

These hidden alleyways (the word means "the alley next door") plunge the culinary curious into an authentic Japan, where smoke-filled diners share the street with izakaya pubs with their old-fashioned charm. There aren't many places to sit, and most stalls only have a counter, but the atmosphere created at these places is unique.

Yomoide Yokocho

商店街

SHÔTENGAI SHOPPING ARCADES

These shopping arcades are found in most towns near the railway station. They're pedestrian alleys, many of them covered, where you'll find lots of small shops selling many different types of food.

A signature shotengaï from Asagaya

コンビニ

KONBINI CONVENIENCE STORES

These 24-hour mini-markets can be found on almost every street corner, offering a snack at any time of the day or night (see p. 160).

デパ地下

DEPACHIKA UPSCALE DEPARTMENT STORES

Located beneath large department stores and entirely dedicated to gourmet foods, they're ideal places to get an idea of what Japanese food is all about. They also provide lots of free samples and take-away dishes to try.

屋台
EATING AT A YATAÏ

These wooden mobile stalls, dating back to the Edo period, moved from temple to temple to offer their dishes during matsuri or festivals. After the war, they reportedly spread to certain devastated cities where everything had to be rebuilt. Today, it's mainly office workers who stop by these small eateries after work, leaning against the counter for a quick meal.

FUKUOKA, THE CAPITAL OF YATAÏ

It is in the city of Fukuoka, on the island of Kyushu in southern Japan, that yataï—which are disappearing elsewhere in Japan—are most numerous. It is estimated that there are over 150 in the city. These small food stalls, recognizable by their lanterns and noren (small fabric curtains), set up along the riverbanks from 6 PM to 2 AM and are usually dismantled each night!

If you want to experience a warm and authentic moment while immersing yourself in Japanese culture, lean against the counter of a yataï. The atmosphere is particularly relaxed, and it's common to socialize with both the owner and other customers.

WHAT CAN YOU EAT AT A YATAÏ?

These small stalls, which can barely fit eight people at the counter, serve mostly popular street food. The most common dishes include ramen, oden, and the famous yakitori (grilled skewers). Each city also offers its own regional specialties: In Fukuoka, several yataï serve mentaiko (spicy cod roe) or tonkotsu ramen (pork bone broth ramen). In Osaka, you are more likely to find yataï selling okonomiyaki (savory pancakes).

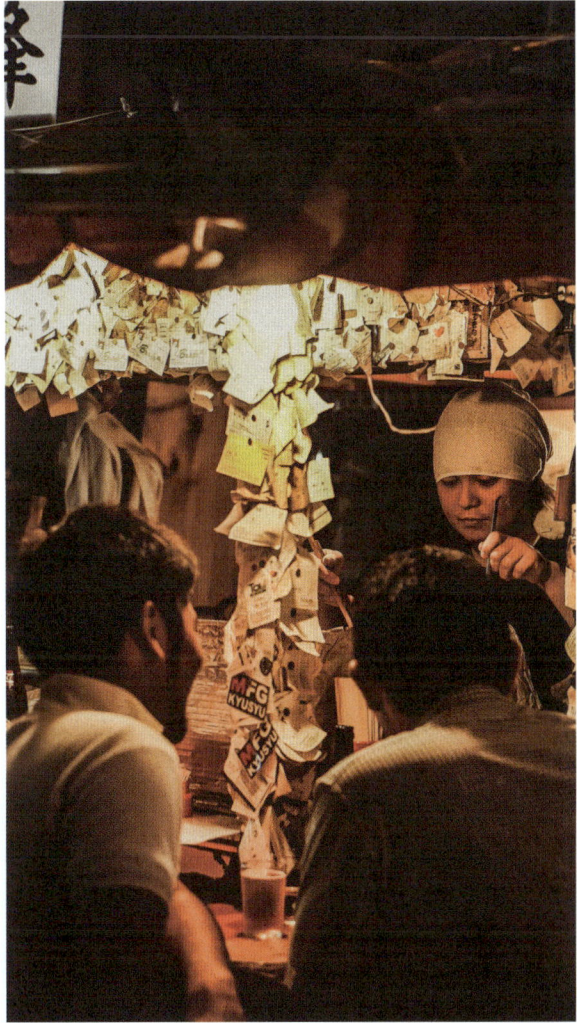

屋台 けいじ

Fukuoka's Yataï Keiji

This stall, entirely built from cypress wood in a traditional manner, aims to preserve and share the yataï culture, which is an essential part of Fukuoka's identity. The young owner, Abe, is passionate about these food stalls and is dedicated to passing on this unique Japanese way of life. Sitting at his counter is a real treat—not just for the delicious food but also for the fascinating stories he shares.

TOKYO STREET FOOD

Tokyo, known for its Michelin-starred restaurants, is also a city where street food is everywhere. In many districts of the capital, rows of food stalls offer a variety of popular dishes to enjoy on the go.

Asakusa Hoppy Street

築地

1. TSUKIJI MARKET

This food market is the largest in Tokyo and the ideal spot to taste different types of Japanese street food—not just seafood-based dishes. Here, you can watch how the famous tamago yaki (Japanese rolled omelet) is made, discover nerimono (fish-based snacks), and enjoy delicious donburi (rice bowls topped with various ingredients).

アメ横

2. AMEYOKO MARKET

A foodie stroll through the vibrant Ameyoko Market is a must. Located in northern Tokyo along the Yamanote Line, this bustling market comes to life at dawn, offering a mix of food stalls, small restaurants with unbeatable prices, and street food vendors. If you're looking for a budget-friendly meal, this is the perfect place!

Ameyoko

浅草

3. ASAKUSA TEMPLE

This historic district is packed with delicious food options. From tiny street stalls to well-established restaurants, the narrow alleys still preserve the atmosphere of old Edo. The main street, Nakamise Dori, leading to the temple, is lined with shops selling Tokyo specialties, while the area around Senso-ji Temple is filled with food stands serving classic yataï dishes, from yakisoba noodles to kakigori.

4. YANAKA GINZA

This shopping street is located in Yanaka, a neighborhood full of old-fashioned small shops where the nostalgic atmosphere of old Tokyo is truly charming. It's an invitation to stroll and indulge in delicious treats among the retro stalls.

5. OMOIDE YOKOCHO

Yakitori is a popular dish often enjoyed in small eateries. To taste these skewers in a post-war Japan ambiance, take a side trip to Omoide Yokocho, literally "Memory Lane," also known as Yakitori Alley.

Omoide Yokocho

6. TOGOSHI GINZA

This is one of the longest shopping streets in Tokyo. Food lovers will be delighted by all the stalls offering various specialties. The atmosphere is lively and authentic, offering a real taste of Japanese daily life.

7. TAKESHITA DORI

In a completely different style, this narrow street immerses you in modern Tokyo, showcasing anime and kawaii culture with its ultra-decorated crêpes. If you're a fan of manga and cosplay, this is the place for you!

浅草

8. SUGAMO JIZO-DORI

In this charmingly old-fashioned shopping street, you'll encounter older women searching for red underwear (a color symbolizing good luck), as well as authentic Japanese flavors. Don't miss visiting on the 4th, 14th, or 24th of each month, when festive stalls line the street.

砂町銀座

9. SUNAMACHI GINZA

There's no better way to experience the typical atmosphere of Japan's popular shopping streets. It's a bit off the beaten path and not very touristy, but this unique spot is definitely worth a visit.

Yurakucho Gado-shita

有楽町 ガード下

10. YURAKUCHO GÂDO-SHITA

Gâdo-shita means "under the tracks" as this nook is indeed located beneath the elevated Yamanote railway line. Near Yurakucho Station, you'll find numerous small eateries where you can sit down for a meal. The sound of passing trains is part of the charm of the location!

OSAKA STREET FOOD

Looking for a unique culinary experience? Head to Osaka in Kansai! Japan's third-largest city is considered the capital of street food and one of the most important gastronomic destinations in the world.

Dotonbori River

Kuromon Market

THE CAPITAL OF JAPANESE STREET FOOD

Osaka's specialties are famous throughout Japan, appreciated by both fine gourmets and street food lovers alike. But the city is especially known as a hub for casual, everyday cuisine. Iconic dishes such as takoyaki, okonomiyaki and kushikatsu are best enjoyed on the go. Simply strolling through the different districts of the city makes it clear—Osaka is a paradise for food lovers!

A GOURMET TOUR THROUGH THE NAMBA DISTRICT

1. Stroll, admire, smell and taste the best street food in the bustling Dotonbori street.

2. Explore Kuromon Market, the true "stomach of Osaka," and grab a seat at one of the in-store tables to enjoy ultrafresh cuisine.

3. Stock up on kitchen tools along Dôguya-suji shopping street, dedicated entirely to cookware and tableware.

4. Experience the vibrant nightlife of the district, which lights up after dark, and dine in one of the many hidden restaurants tucked away in the small alleys.

黒門市場
KUROMON MARKET

A true culinary hub of Osaka, this colorful market welcomes nearly 20,000 visitors daily! You won't be alone in sampling the many delicacies offered at the various stalls, whether for takeout or to enjoy right there. A must-visit destination for an unforgettable foodie experience!

道頓堀
DOTONBORI

Located in the Namba district, this bustling street is mesmerizing with its energy and extravagance. Giant 3D signs decorate the facades of countless restaurants lining this food-centric district. Watching skilled chefs create perfectly round takoyaki is fascinating—and tasting these local specialties is even better!

Dotonbori

新世界
SHINSEKAI

Built in the early 20th century, inspired by both Paris and New York, Shinsekai—meaning "New World"—was once a thriving entertainment district before World War II. After decades of decline, it has now become one of Osaka's most visited areas, renowned for its retro atmosphere and budget-friendly gourmet delights.

Shinsekai

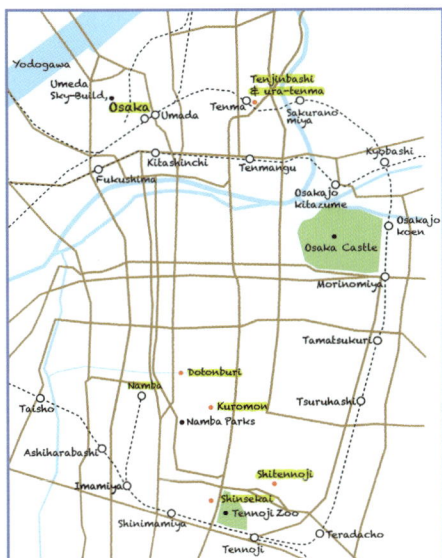

裏天満
URA-TENMA ARCADE

Just minutes from Tenma Station and Tenjinbashi—the city's longest covered shopping street—Ura-Tenma ("Back of Tenma") is a collection of small alleys where food stalls, yatais and tiny post-war-style bars coexist. Still largely undiscovered by tourists, it's the perfect spot to share a drink with locals.

KYOTO STREET FOOD

A former imperial capital, the city is a true treasure with its temples and gardens, historic districts and rich culture. However, while it's known as a refined gastronomic city, Kyoto is also full of places where street food thrives, blending tradition and modernity.

Nishiki Market

Ninenzaka

錦市場 NISHIKI MARKET

The covered Nishiki Market is the gastronomic center of Kyoto. It's an essential stop for all food lovers eager to discover new flavors. Visitors shouldn't hesitate to try the local specialties offered at the many stalls. Here, most shops have a long history and are passed down from generation to generation.

東山 HIGASHIYAMA

To the east of the city, Higashiyama offers a culinary stroll not to be missed. Between Kiyomizu-dera Temple and Gion, the geisha district, passing through the historic alleys of Sannenzaka and Ninenzaka, there's no shortage of stalls selling traditional sweets, dango, matcha ice cream and other delights. Wandering through this district will awaken your taste buds while immersing you in its rich cultural heritage.

TEMPLE FLEA MARKETS

Some temples are lively places where large flea markets are held on fixed dates each month. On these occasions, you can browse for treasures and perhaps find a beautiful kimono, but you can also take a break and sample Kyoto's top street food specialties at the numerous stalls set up for the event.

Here are the three main flea markets in Kyoto:

TEZUKURI-ICHI—Location: Chion-ji Temple
Date: 15th of each month

KOBO-SAN—Location: Toji Temple
Date: 21st of each month

TENJIN-SAN—Location: Kitano Tenmangu Temple
Date: 25th of each month

KYOTO SPECIALTIES

抹茶 MATCHA (GREEN TEA)

Uji, located south of the city, is renowned for its high-quality matcha tea production. Kyoto is the perfect place to enjoy this green treasure, available both as a drink and in pastries.

豆腐 TOFU

With its 1,600 temples and 400 shrines, the former imperial capital has developed a unique vegetarian culinary culture. Tofu is a staple here, particularly in the form of yuba, the delicate skin that forms on soy milk, or yudofu, a comforting tofu hot pot.

奥丹
Okutan Tofu Restaurant

In front of this renowned restaurant, famous for its refined tofu cuisine and located in the Kiyomizu-dera district, you can buy one of my favorite snacks in Kyoto: tofu manju. This small savory bun is filled with okara, the soybean pulp left after tofu production, along with vegetables, creating a delicate and satisfying treat that can be enjoyed at any time of the day.

鯖ずし SABA-ZUSHI

This Kyoto-style mackerel sushi is pressed rather than hand-shaped like most sushi. The fish is first pickled in vinegar and salted, giving it a light cure before being pressed onto sushi rice.

タコ玉子 TAKO TAMAGO

These mini caramelized octopuses, glazed with a slightly sweet soy sauce and stuffed with quail eggs (tako means "octopus" and tamago means "egg"), are one of Nishiki Market's signature curiosities and can now be found at many street food stalls throughout Kyoto.

YAKITORI

Yakitori, literally meaning "grilled chicken," is undoubtedly the star of Japanese street food. These small, flavorful skewers are grilled over a barbecue and dipped in a sweet-savory sauce, not surprisingly called yakitori sauce, to give them a luscious glaze.

焼き鳥屋台

YAKITORI STALLS

Yakitori is a highly popular dish, often enjoyed at the many yatai (see pages 12–13) located in the bustling districts of major cities. However, these delicate charcoal-grilled skewers are also widely enjoyed in izakaya (Japanese-style tapas bars).

焼き鳥屋台 Yakitori Yatai

YAKITORI ALLEY

To experience these skewers in a setting reminiscent of post-war Japan, visit Omoide Yokocho, also known as Yakitori Alley. Just a few streets west of the bustling Shinjuku Station, this nighttime stroll will introduce you to another side of one of Tokyo's most vibrant districts.

白ネギ
Shironegi
Leek

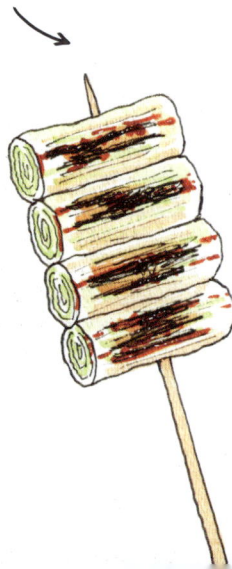

ししとう
Shishitou
Green Peppers

VARIETIES OF YAKITORI

Traditionally, yakitori is made with chicken, but many variations exist using vegetables and other proteins such as beef or duck.

若鶏
Wakabori
Chicken Thigh

とりかわ
Torikawa
Chicken Skin

アスパラベーコン
Asparagus Bacon
Asparagus Wrapped in Bacon

しいたけ
shitake
Shiitake Mushrooms

つくね
Tsukune
Minced Chicken Meatballs

ねぎま
Negima
Chicken Thigh and Leek

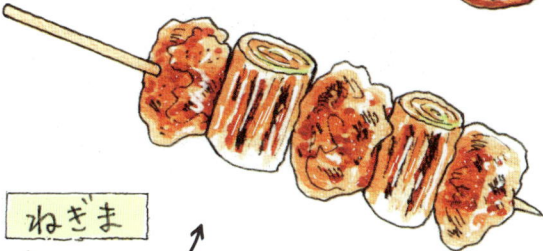

豚バラ
Butabara
Pork Belly

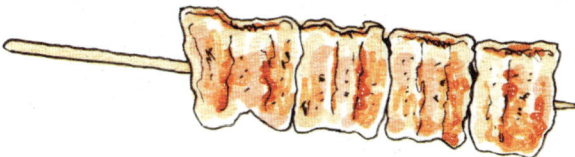

YAKITORI SKEWERS

These skewers can be cooked on a stovetop grill, but if you can, try cooking them over a wood fire, which brings out the characteristic flavor of yakitori.

とりかわ
← Torikawa
Chicken skin

How to Make Yakitori:

CUTTING: Chicken (or vegetables) are cut into bite-sized pieces for easy eating.

SKEWERING: The pieces are then placed onto bamboo skewers.

COOKING: The skewers are grilled on the barbecue.

SEASONING: As they cook, the skewers are dipped in yakitori sauce (which can also be applied with a brush). Some pieces may be seasoned with salt, instead of yakitori sauce, at the end of cooking.

YAKITORI SAUCE

This delicious sauce, which gives the succulent grilled tidbits their caramelized glaze, is rich in flavor. It's easy to buy it in bottles in Asian grocery stores or supermarkets, but don't hesitate to make it yourself using this recipe.

Makes: Just less than 1 cup (200 ml)
Prep time: 10 min
Cooking time: 15 min

- ⅔ cup (150 ml) soy sauce
- ½ cup (120 ml) sake
- 5 tablespoons mirin
- 3 tablespoons caster sugar
- ½ teaspoon chicken bouillon powder (or ½ bouillon cube)

Pour all the ingredients into a saucepan, bring to the boil, stirring to dissolve the sugar and stock, then turn down the heat and simmer for about 15 minutes over low heat until syrupy.

TIP
This sauce can keep up to 1 week in a jar in the refrigerator.

NEGIMA YAKITORI

This variety of chicken and leek (called negi in Japanese) skewer is undoubtedly the most popular type of yakitori, but you can also use other vegetables, such as peppers or asparagus.

Makes: 12 skewers
Prep time: 20 min
Cooking time: 8 min

- **1 lb (450 g) chicken thighs**
- **4 baby leeks or large green onions**
- **Just less than ½ cup (100 ml) yakitori sauce (see p. 27)**
- **12 skewers**

Wash the leeks and cut them into 1½-inch (4-cm) sections.

Bone the chicken thighs and cut the meat into bite-sized cubes.

Alternate the chicken cubes and leek sections on 12 wooden skewers.

Heat up the barbecue. Grill the skewers for about 6 to 8 minutes, turning them and dipping them regularly in the sauce (about 3 times) during cooking.

At the end of the cooking time, the skewers should be golden brown and dipped in the sauce one last time before serving.

CHICKEN PARTS

In Japan, all parts of the chicken are used, including the skin and cartilage, but the prized part is the thigh. For grilling, avoid using the breast, which dries out during cooking, and opt for boneless thighs, which are much juicier.

ねぎま
Negima

TIP
Cut the chicken pieces to the same size to ensure even cooking, and use very thin leeks (in Japan, negi is between the size of a spring onion and a leek) so that they're sufficiently cooked.

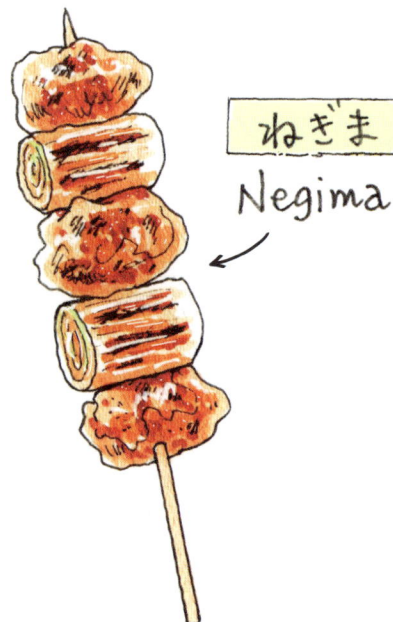

コツ

GRILLED SCALLOPS

The Japanese love their seafood! Scallops are no exception, mainly coming from the island of Hokkaido in the far north. This simple recipe for scallops with ponzu sauce captures the true essence of Japanese cuisine. An even simpler preparation features the scallops in a combination of butter and soy sauce.

For 8 scallops
Preparation: 20 min
Cooking: 5 to 6 min

- **8 fresh scallops**
- **3½ tablespoon unsalted butter**
- **⅓ cup (80 ml) ponzu sauce (see below)**
- **Freshly ground pepper**

Rinse the scallops thoroughly, patting them dry. Distribute the butter on top and season with pepper.

Heat the barbecue and cook the scallops for about 4 minutes.

Add the ponzu sauce and continue cooking for 1 to 2 more minutes (the sauce should be hot but not boiling).

Prepare the sauce the day before. Place all the ingredients in a jar. Close the jar and let the flavors infuse in the refrigerator overnight. Strain the sauce the next day.

PONZU SAUCE

For 1 cup (250 ml) of ponzu sauce:
- **1 small handful of dried bonito flakes (or 1 large dried shiitake mushroom)**
- **1 tablespoon sugar**
- **2-inch (5-cm) square piece of dried kombu seaweed**
- **⅔ cup (150 ml) soy sauce**
- **2 teaspoons lemon juice**
- **¼ cup (60 ml) orange juice**
- **4 tablespoons mirin (or sweet cooking sherry)**

This citrus and soy sauce blend adds a refreshing touch to dishes. It's often paired with fish or tofu but complements white meats and vegetables, especially in hot pots.

Pour all the ingredients into a saucepan.

Bring to a boil, stirring to dissolve the sugar and broth, then let it simmer over low heat for about 15 minutes until it reaches a syrupy consistency.

TIP
Ponzu sauce can be bought in Asian grocery stores or supermarkets, but you can also make it at home, where it will keep for two weeks in a jar in the refrigerator.

WAGYU KUSHI SKEWERS

Wagyu has become synonymous with melt-in-your-mouth beef, an incredibly tender and flavorful treat. Its main characteristic is its abundant marbling, which gives it an exceptionally tender texture and a delicate buttery flavor.

For 4 skewers
Preparation: 10 min
Cooking: 2 to 3 min
Resting time: 2 min

- **14 oz (400 g) of wagyu beef (fillet, ribeye, or sirloin)**
- **Salt and freshly ground pepper, to taste**
- **Wasabi (optional)**

Cut the meat into evenly sized bite-sized pieces.

Thread the meat onto 4 wooden skewers.

Heat up the barbecue. Season the skewers with salt and pepper. Grill them for about 2 to 3 minutes, depending on their thickness, turning them halfway through cooking. Once cooked, let them rest for 2 minutes before serving, optionally with a light smear of wasabi.

TIP
Wagyu is expensive, but you can easily use any other well-marbled beef.

YAKINIKU SAUCE

For about ½ cup (125 ml) of sauce
Preparation: 5 min
Cooking: 3 min

- **½ cup (100 g) grated onion**
- **5 tablespoons soy sauce**
- **5 tablespoons mirin**
- **3 tablespoons sake**
- **2 tablespoons granulated sugar**
- **1 grated garlic clove**

As a skewer, wagyu is prepared simply with minimal seasoning to fully enjoy the quality of the meat. However, if you opt for a more common cut of beef, you can serve it with a pop of yakiniku sauce.

Heat the grated onion in a saucepan over high heat until the water released by the onion starts to boil. Then add the soy sauce, mirin, sake and sugar, and let it boil for 1 minute. Remove from the heat and stir in the grated garlic.

YAKI-IMO

Japanese sweet potatoes, satsuma-imo, are tender and naturally sweet, almost candied. Grilled in their skins (yaki-imo means "grilled potato"), they make a perfect snack, enjoyed from street vendor stalls across Japan during the autumn and winter.

Yakiimo 焼き芋

Preparing satsuma-imo is incredibly simple—it's just a matter of choosing the right cooking method! Charcoal grilling gives the flesh a unique flavor, but here are a few different techniques:

Grilled Over Charcoal:

Heat up the barbecue. Wash, dry and lightly prick the sweet potatoes with a fork to allow steam to escape. Grill them for about 40 minutes, turning occasionally. The skin should become crispy without burning. Once cooked, let them rest for a few minutes before eating.

In the Oven:

Preheat the oven to 350°F (180°C). Wash the sweet potatoes, prick them lightly with a fork (to prevent them from bursting in the oven) and bake them for 1 hour. Let them rest for a few minutes before enjoying.

Steamed:

Wash and cut the sweet potatoes in half. Heat water in a steamer. Place the sweet potatoes in the steaming basket, cover and cook for about 30 minutes (test for doneness by piercing them with a knife).

YAKI-IMO VENDORS

It carries a sense of nostalgia because, although some street vendors still walk through certain neighborhoods calling out "Yaki-imooo!" (grilled potatoes) to attract customers, they're becoming increasingly rare.

NOTE

Originally from Kagoshima, these basic favorites are also used in sweet dishes, often as a substitute for anko (red bean paste), such as in taiyaki (see p. 182) filled with sweet potato or in yōkan (a traditional jelly-like dessert).

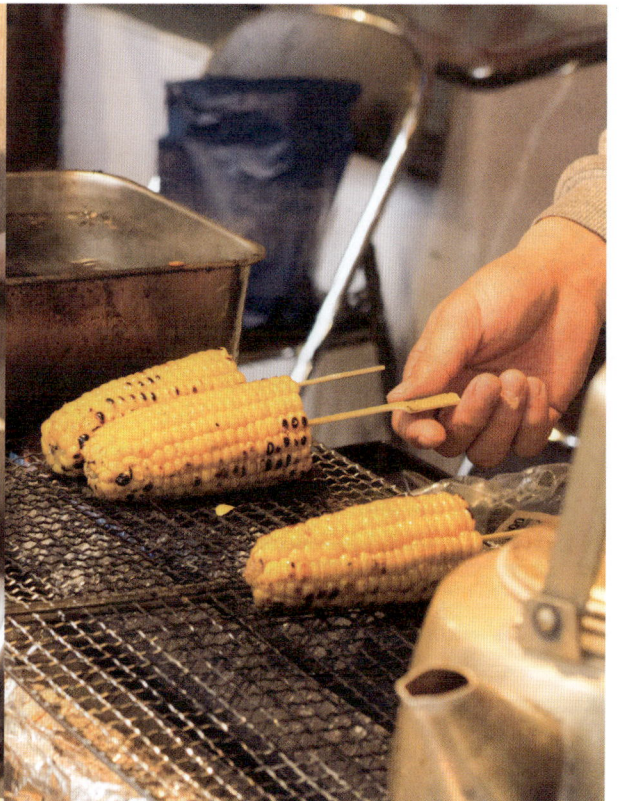

YAKI TŌMOROKOSHI

In summer, many matsuri stalls (p. 48) offer this simple recipe for grilled soy-glazed corn (tōmorokoshi means "corn" and yaki means "grilled").

For 4 people
Preparation: 10 min
Cooking: 15 min

- **4 fresh ears of corn**

For the Sauce:
- **3 tablespoons soy sauce**
- **2 tablespoons mirin**
- **1 teaspoon sugar**

Husk the corn. Cut off the stem of each cob and steam them for 8 minutes.

Place the corn on bamboo skewers.

Pour all the Sauce ingredients into a small saucepan and heat over low heat until the sugar is fully dissolved.

Heat up the barbecue. Brush the corn with the Sauce and grill for about 5 minutes, turning them 2 or 3 times and brushing with more Sauce each time. At the end of cooking, give them a final coat of Sauce before serving.

NOTE

Instead of the soy-based sauce, some vendors offer an alternative by brushing the grilled corn with a mixture of miso and butter—a wonderful combination!

TIP
If you don't have a barbecue, you can make this recipe in a pan. In this case, cut the corn in half lengthwise and cook it in the pan with a little knob of butter until it's slightly browned. Pour the sauce over at the end of cooking, rolling the pieces around to coat them well.

GRILLED SENBEI RICE CRACKERS

These crispy rice crackers can be either savory or sweet, grilled or fried. In the savory version, they're often seasoned with soy sauce and wrapped in a sheet of nori or sprinkled with sesame seeds. There are still traditional shops where senbei are grilled on-site, releasing an aroma that's irresistible and attracts passersby!

For about 20 senbei
Preparation: 10 min
Cooking: 8 min

- **1 cup (180 g) cooked Japanese rice (see p. 123)**
- **2 tablespoons sesame seeds**
- **2 tablespoons soy sauce**

In a bowl, mix all the ingredients together, mashing the rice grains.

Form a ball and roll it out between two sheets of parchment paper, just as you would with dough, until it reaches a thickness of about ⅛ in (3 mm).

Place the flattened dough in the microwave and dry it at 500 watts for 3 minutes, keeping it in between the two sheets of parchment paper. Flip the dough and microwave again for another 3 minutes.

Remove the top parchment sheet and continue microwaving in 30-second intervals until the dough becomes golden and crispy.

Throughout the cooking process, before restarting the microwave, wipe off any water droplets that may have collected on the bottom.

Carefully cut the dough into squares.

TIP
You can shape the dough into circles about 3 inches (8 cm) in diameter before cooking to make them look more authentic.

NOTE

Microwaving is the fastest method, but you can also dry and grill the crackers (season the cooked rice with salt instead of soy sauce to prevent additional moisture from forming), then flatten it in the same way as in the recipe. Remove the top parchment sheet and let the dough dry for 24 hours. The next day, cut it into squares and grill them over a barbecue until they begin to brown, then brush them with soy sauce. Alternatively, you can fry them in oil instead of grilling them.

TAKOYAKI

Takoyaki, meaning "grilled octopus," are grilled balls of egg batter filled with small bits of octopus. This Osaka specialty has become a symbol of Japanese street food.

Mix the Batter ingredients in a bowl.

Heat the takoyaki pan and grease it with oil. Pour the Batter into the molds, then distribute the Filling in the center of each portion.

At the halfway point (about 2 minutes), use a metal skewer to flip each ball. This takes some practice!

Enjoy the takoyaki seasoned with takoyaki sauce, Kewpie mayonnaise and ao-nori seaweed flakes.

Variations:

• Replace the octopus with shrimp (easier to find).

• Swap the octopus for diced chorizo for a spicy version!

• Add cubes of Emmental cheese for a melty center.

A Few Tips:

1. To make takoyaki at home, you must have a takoyaki pan!

2. Use two pointed skewers to rotate the takoyaki balls.

3. Fill the takoyaki pan generously with the Batter and Filling, as the excess Batter helps complete the sphere when flipped.

4. Don't overcook the takoyaki—they should be golden on the outside but still soft inside!

For about 20 takoyaki
Preparation: 15 min
Cooking: 5 min

For the Batter:
- 2 eggs
- ¾ cup (100 g) flour
- 1¼ cups (300 ml) dashi broth or fish stock
- ½ tablespoon soy sauce
- 1 teaspoon baking powder
- A drizzle of vegetable oil
- A pinch of salt

For the Filling:
- ⅓ cup (80 g) cooked octopus or shrimp, diced
- 1 tablespoon pickled ginger (beni shōga)
- 1 green onion, finely chopped

For serving:
- Takoyaki sauce (or tonkatsu sauce, see page 110)
- Kewpie mayonnaise
- Seaweed flakes (ao-nori) or katsuobushi

たこ焼き Takoyaki

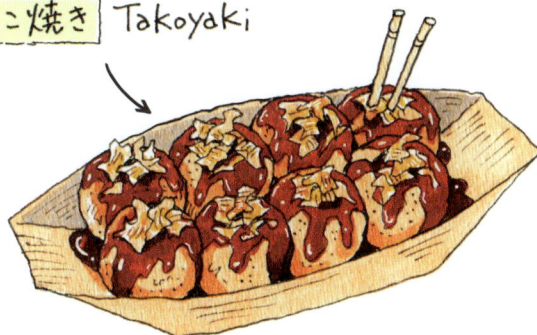

YAKISOBA FRIED NOODLES

Noodles, originally from China, are a staple of Japanese street food. They're most often stir-fried with vegetables and meat, then coated in a thick, slightly sweet sauce called, not surprisingly, yakisoba sauce.

For 4 people
Preparation: 15 min
Cooking: 10 min

- **1⅓ lbs (600 g) fresh yakisoba noodles (available in Asian grocery stores) or Chinese egg noodles or cooked spaghetti**
- **¼ lb (125 g) thin unsalted pork belly, cut into strips**
- **1 onion, thinly sliced**
- **4 fresh shiitake mushrooms, thinly sliced**
- **8 green cabbage leaves, sliced**
- **8 tablespoons yakisoba sauce (available in bottles in Asian grocery stores)**

For Garnishing:
- **Pickled ginger (beni shōga)**
- **Powdered seaweed (ao-nori)**

焼きそば Yakisoba

Rinse the yakisoba noodles under hot water and drain them.

In a pan, heat a little oil and sauté the pork belly strips and sliced onions. Add the shiitake mushrooms, then the cabbage cut into pieces.

Add the noodles and stir-fry for 1 minute. Pour in the yakisoba sauce, making sure all the ingredients are well coated.

Divide the mixture onto plates. Garnish with strips of red pickled ginger and sprinkle with ao-nori seaweed powder. Serve immediately.

TIP
You can replace yakisoba sauce with tonkatsu or okonomiyaki sauce. You can also mix barbecue sauce with a touch of vinegar or Worcestershire sauce to season your stir-fried noodles.

OKONOMIYAKI

The term "okonomiyaki" could be translated as "grill whatever you like." It's often referred to as a stuffed pancake, but it's so much more! This iconic dish from Osaka has a variation in Hiroshima that includes noodles. This is the version I'm sharing with you here.

Serves: 4 people (2 pancakes)
Cooking: 15 min
Preparation: 15 min

- 9 oz (250 g) dried yakisoba noodles or ramen noodles
- 1 cup (100 g) green cabbage, finely shredded
- 2 green onions
- 1 cup (60 g) snow peas
- 6 thin slices of bacon (6 oz/170 g)
- 2 eggs
- 1 heaping tablespoon potato or cornstarch
- ⅔ cup (80 g) flour
- ⅓ cup + 1 tablespoon (100 ml) dashi broth or chicken stock
- Sunflower oil, for cooking

For serving:
- Okonomiyaki sauce or yakisoba sauce (available in Asian grocery stores)
- Kewpie mayonnaise or regular mayonnaise
- Katsuobushi (dried bonito flakes, optional)

In a bowl, mix the flour, starch and dashi or chicken broth until you get a smooth consistency. Refrigerate.

Meanwhile, cook the noodles in boiling water according to the package instructions. Rinse them with cold water and drain.

Wash and finely chop the cabbage and green onions. Wash the snow peas.

Oil the teppanyaki (or griddle) with a paper towel and heat it over medium heat. Pour half of the batter, spreading it into a pancake shape with a spatula. Top with half of the cabbage, green onions, snow peas and 3 slices of bacon. Cook for 3 minutes.

At the same time, next to the pancake, spread half of the cooked noodles into a circle of the same size. Cook for 3 minutes, then flip them.

Crack 1 egg onto the griddle and spread it out with a spatula. Once it starts to set on top, place the noodle circle over it, then cover with the flipped pancake (so the noodles are now between the egg and the bacon). Flip everything again so the egg is on top and cook for another 3 minutes. Repeat the same process for the second pancake with the remaining ingredients.

Brush the pancakes with okonomiyaki sauce and Japanese mayonnaise. Optionally, garnish with katsuobushi just before serving.

Okonomiyaki
お好み焼き

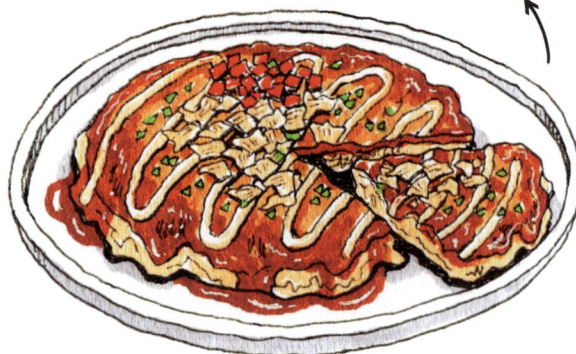

TIP
Okonomiyaki sauce can be purchased at Asian grocery stores. You can substitute it with yakisoba sauce or Worcestershire sauce (available in supermarkets).

MATSURI FESTIVALS

Matsuri are popular festivals, often linked to Shinto celebrations, held throughout Japan. They usually take place in summer, where people dress in yukata (summer kimonos), enjoy delicious treats from food stalls and marvel at the stunning hanabi (fireworks) bursting overhead.

Matsuri at Hanazono Shrine, Shinjuku

Food stalls at Okunitama Jinja

露天商 ROTENSHŌ FOOD STALLS

During matsuri, food stalls called **rotensho** offer dishes such as **yakisoba** (p. 44), **takoyaki** (p. 43), **okonomiyaki** (p. 46), **ramune** (Japanese lemonade, p. 194) and **kakigori** (p. 174). Unlike traditional yatai, which are permanent street stalls, rotensho are temporary stands set up only for the matsuri.

花火 HANABI

Fireworks are the symbol of summer matsuri. People gather to admire them while enjoying the cooler evening air, often bringing an uchiwa (a traditional fan) to stay cool.

You can also see many fireworks displays during New Year celebrations.

神輿 MIKOSHI

Many matsuri, often linked to Shinto celebrations, feature processions of floats or portable shrines (mikoshi) being carried toward temples. The most famous is the Gion Matsuri in Kyoto, which takes place in July.

季節 THE JAPANESE SEASONS

Like an ode to the fleeting nature of the present and the passage of time, Japanese festivals and celebrations are often tied to the seasons. They provide an opportunity for families and friends to come together to celebrate nature, ancestors and their collective heritage.

Whether it's for cherry blossom season, moon viewing or honoring children and ancestors, these moments of communal celebration create unique experiences and treasured memories for family and friends.

THE MATSURI CALENDAR

The Japanese celebrate festivals and rituals throughout the year. These events offer the chance to experience a lively atmosphere and taste different culinary specialties from the many food stalls set up for the occasion. Here is an overview of some matsuri you won't want to miss.

SAKURA MATSURI

LOCATION: All across Japan

Late March—Early April

Spring in Japan is closely associated with sakura—cherry blossoms. Their fleeting bloom is celebrated during hanami, which means "flower viewing." During this time, many locations hold festivities with food stalls so people can enjoy picnics under the blooming trees. One of the most vibrant spots in Tokyo is Ueno Park.

KURAYAMI MATSURI

LOCATION: Fuchu, West of Tokyo

April 30—May 6

The "Festival of Darkness" takes place at Okunitama Shrine. The festival features parades of floats, shamisen and taiko drum performances, horse races, and a central avenue lined with numerous food stalls to delight visitors.

KAZAGURUMA
風車

GION MATSURI

LOCATION: Kyoto

July

Held at Yasaka Shrine, this is one of Japan's most important festivals. It lasts the entire month of July, with two major highlights: grand float processions on July 17 and July 24. For the best festive experience, visit on one of the three nights leading up to the first parade.

AWA ODORI

LOCATION: Tokushima, Shikoku Island

August 12—15

Historically, this was a religious festival honoring the spirits of ancestors. Today, Awa Odori, also known as the "Dance of Fools," is Japan's largest and most famous folk dance festival.

KOENJI AWA ODORI

LOCATION: Koenji, Tokyo

Late August

To the beat of drums, thousands of dancers flood the streets of this lively Tokyo neighborhood. It's energetic, exhilarating and even hypnotic. The entire area transforms into a massive celebration for two days.

OMEN お面

HANABI

LOCATION: Throughout Japan

(Fireworks Festivals) Summer

Here are some of Japan's major hanabi (fireworks festivals):

- **Sumidagawa, Tokyo (last Saturday of July)**
- **Nagaoka, Niigata Prefecture (August 1–3)**
- **Kumano, Mie Prefecture (August 17)**
- **Omagari, Akita Prefecture (4th Saturday of August)**

TENJIN MATSURI

LOCATION: Osaka

July 24 & 25

This major festival celebrates learning and scholarship. You can watch magnificent processions of floats and boats, followed by a breathtaking fireworks display at night.

OESHIKI MATSURI

LOCATION: Ikegami, South Tokyo

October 11–13

This festival commemorates the death of a famous Buddhist monk and attracts nearly 300,000 visitors each year to Ikegami Honmonji Temple.

OSHŌGATSU

LOCATION: All across Japan

New Year's Festival

New Year's is undoubtedly the most important celebration of the year. As the new year begins, Japanese people visit temples to listen to the 108 bell chimes, and on New Year's Day, large crowds gather at major temples for their first prayer of the year. Even small neighborhood temples come to life with festivities and food stalls. During the New Year period, you can also witness the traditional mochi-making process, where rice cakes are pounded—a symbol of happiness and prosperity.

ALL ABOUT RAMEN

The history of ramen traces back to China, where these wheat noodles originated. The first ramen restaurants in Japan appeared in the port city of Yokohama, south of Tokyo. However, this simple and comforting dish spread widely in the early 20th century, following the Kanto earthquake. Many chefs who had lost their workplaces in the massive fires began serving bowls of ramen from small mobile stalls called yataï.

ネギ
Negi

のり
Nori

メンマ
Menma

煮玉子
Nitamago

チャーシュー
Chashu

麺
Men

スープ
Soup

WHAT MAKES UP A BOWL OF RAMEN?

1. THE BROTH
2. THE NOODLES
3. THE TOPPINGS

スープ

THE BROTH

The broth consists of a base stock (pork, chicken, fish), a tare seasoning (soy sauce, salt, miso) and either fat or oil. Here are the four main types of ramen broth:

SHOYU RAMEN: Broth seasoned with soy sauce

MISO RAMEN: Miso seasoned broth

SHIO RAMEN: Broth seasoned with salt

TONKOTSU RAMEN: A rich pork bone broth

Shoyu Ramen

醤油ラーメン

札幌 みそラーメン
Sapporo Miso Ramen

Shio Ramen
塩ラーメン

豚骨ラーメン
Tonkotsu Ramen

麺 THE NOODLES

A good ramen restaurant makes its own wheat noodles. The shape, thickness and texture vary depending on the region.

FUTO CHIJIRE MEN: Thick, wavy noodles

HOSSO CHIJIRE MEN: Thin, wavy noodles

HOSSO MEN STRAIGHT: Thin, straight noodles

HIRA STRAIGHT: Flat, straight noodles

細麺ストレート
Thin Straight
Thin noodles

太ちぢれ麺
Thick Curly
Thick wavy noodles

細ちぢれ麺
Thin Curly
Thin wavy noodles

平ストレート麺
Flat Straight
Thick noodles

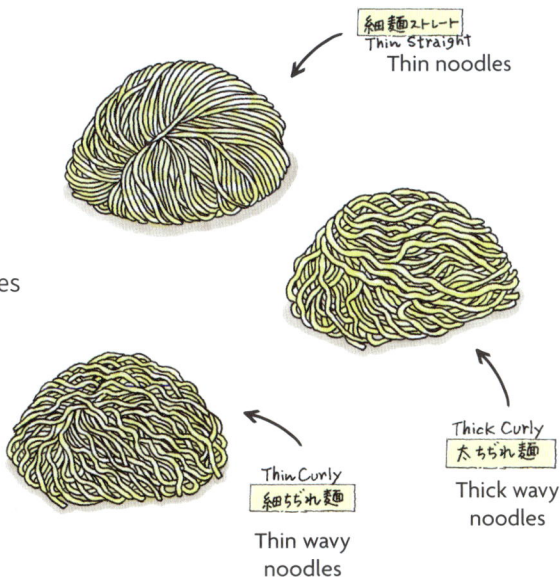

チャーシュー chashu

のり Nori

きくらげ Kikurage

煮玉子 Nitamago

紅しょうが Beni Syoga

かまぼこ Kamaboki

メンマ Menma

わかめ Wakame

ゴマ Goma

ナルト Naruto

コーン Corn

ほうれん草 Hourenso

もやし Moyashi

ネギ Negi

バター Butter

トッピング

THE TOPPINGS

There is a wide variety of ramen, due to the different topping combinations.

CHASHU: Braised pork (see recipe p. 58)

NORI: Seaweed sheet that adds an umami, oceanic flavor

KIKURAGE: Black mushrooms (also known as wood ear mushrooms)

NITAMAGO: Soft-boiled or marinated egg

BENI SHŌGA: Pickled red ginger

KAMABOKO: Japanese fish cake (surimi)

MENMA: Fermented bamboo shoots

WAKAME: Seaweed used in soups or salads

GOMA: Sesame seeds

NARUTO: Swirled fish cake (surimi)

CORN: Cooked corn kernels

HORENSO: Spinach

MOYASHI: Blanched bean sprouts

NEGI: Green onions

BUTTER: A rich addition, often used in miso ramen

RAMEN BROTH

Ramen broth is made by combining three elements:

1. THE BASE BROTH, unsalted, made from pork, chicken or fish

2. THE TARE SAUCE, which defines the main flavor of the broth (soy sauce, miso or salt)

3. THE SEASONED OIL, which adds richness and depth to the dish

1. THE BASE BROTH

Serves: 6-8
Preparation: 10 min
Cooking: 1 hr 30 min

Chicken Broth:
- 1 medium chicken carcass
- 2 chicken wings
- 2 green onions
- 4 crushed garlic cloves
- 1½-in (4-cm) piece of ginger, crushed
- 12⅔ cups (3 l) of dashi broth (available in Asian grocery stores or see recipe on p. 88)

Place the chicken carcass and wings in a large pot, cover them with water, bring it all to a boil and cook for 1 minute. Drain.

In a large pot, add the blanched chicken pieces along with the remaining ingredients. Pour in the broth. Cover and bring to a boil. Skim off any impurities. Let simmer for 1½ hours over low heat without a lid. Strain the broth, and it's ready!

Serves: 6-8
Preparation: 15 min
Cooking: 4 hr

Tonkotsu Broth:
- 4½ lbs (2 kg) pork bones
- 1 piece kombu (about 4 in/ 10 cm square)
- 1 baby leek or large green onion, cut into 3 pieces
- 4 garlic cloves, crushed
- 1½-in (4-cm) piece ginger, sliced
- 1 medium onion (5 oz/150 g)

Place the pork bones in a large pot, cover them with water, bring it to a boil and cook for 5 minutes. Drain, rinse the bones and break them roughly with a hammer to release the marrow during cooking.

In a large pot, add the blanched bones along with the remaining ingredients. Pour in 12⅔ cups (3 l) of water. Cover and bring to a boil. Skim off any impurities. Let simmer for 4 hours over low heat without a lid. Strain the broth.

Quick Broth:
- **1 chicken bouillon cube**
- **1 teaspoon dashi broth powder (available in Asian grocery stores or see recipe on p. 88)**
- **2 green onions, roughly chopped**

Place all ingredients in a large pot with 12⅔ cups (3 l) of water, bring to a boil and cook for 10 minutes.

2. THE TARE SAUCE

RECIPE

SOY SAUCE BASE: This is the most common type. If you prepare chashu pork (see p. 58), you don't need to make a separate tare sauce—just use the cooking sauce from the meat.

In a saucepan, combine: 3 crushed garlic cloves, ¾ in (2 cm) sliced ginger, ⅖ cup (100 ml) soy sauce, 2 tbsp (30 ml) mirin, ⅖ cup (100 ml) sake, ⅖ cup (100 ml) water and 3 tbsp sugar. Bring to a boil.

MISO BASE: In a bowl, mix: 8 tbsp miso, 3 tbsp mirin, 3 tbsp sake and 1 tbsp sugar until dissolved. Then add 1 small grated garlic clove and 1 tsp grated ginger. Mix well.

3. THE SEASONED OIL

RECIPE

The seasoned oil can be vegetable-based (sesame oil, chili oil rayu) or animal-based (rendered pork or duck fat).

If using animal fat, heat it before incorporating it into the broth.

The amount depends on your preference, but the oil content should remain relatively low (about 1 to 2 teaspoons per bowl). For chili oil, just a few drops are enough.

CHASHU PORK

This braised pork is one of the key toppings for a bowl of ramen. The recipe here creates incredibly tender meat as well as a flavorful condiment, the tare sauce, that will deliciously season your broth.

Serves: About 6 people
Preparation: 15 min
Cooking: 2 hr 30 min
Resting Time: 4 hours

- 2¼ lbs (1 kg) fresh pork belly (without the skin)
- ¾ cup (200 ml) soy sauce
- ⅔ cup (150 ml) sake
- 3 tablespoons mirin
- ¾ cup (200 ml) water
- 4 tablespoons sugar
- 6 garlic cloves, crushed
- 1½ in (4 cm) ginger, sliced
- 4 green onions, cut into quarters

Step-by-Step Chashu Preparation:

Roll the pork belly tightly and tie it with kitchen twine.

Sear the pork on all sides in a large pot over high heat for about 15 minutes. Add the remaining ingredients. Bring to a boil, skim off any impurities, reduce the heat, then cover and let it simmer for 2 hours, turning the meat every 30 minutes.

Reduce the cooking sauce: Remove the lid, take out the meat and let the sauce reduce for 10 to 15 minutes. Return the meat to the pot, coat it well with the sauce and let everything cool before refrigerating for at least 4 hours.

Final steps: Drain the meat, reserving the cooking sauce—this is your tare sauce. Slice the meat into thin pieces. Reheat it in the tare sauce, in the ramen broth or use a butane torch to give it a slightly grilled flavor.

NOTE

You can cook the chashu without rolling the pork belly, keeping it flat instead. If using this method, cut the pork belly to about 2½ in (6 cm) wide. Reduce the cooking time to 1 hr 20 min, instead of 2 hr.

TIP
Purists prefer unsmoked and unsalted pork belly, which results in ultra-tender meat but is naturally rich in fat. For a leaner version, opt for pork shoulder instead.

RAMEN STANDS

It was after the Tokyo earthquake of 1923 that yatai began to spread throughout the partially destroyed city. The trend then became widespread across Japan in the aftermath of World War II. One of the most common dishes served in street food stalls is a bowl of ramen noodles, as it provides a warm, complete meal—perfect for chilly evenings. Today, the number of yatai has significantly decreased, but these stalls remain an ideal place to experience Japanese culture, chat with the owner and interact with fellow diners.

FUKUOKA, THE YATAI CAPITAL

Every region and yatai has its own specialty. But if you want to experience a ramen yatai, visit Fukuoka, the main city on Kyushu Island, which has made these street stalls a symbol of the city. You can find them mainly in three districts:

1. TENJIN—The busiest district in Fukuoka, home to shopping streets, malls and restaurants.

2. NAKASU—An island across from Tenjin on the other side of the Nakagawa River, famous for its vibrant nightlife, with numerous restaurants and bars.

3. NAGAHAMA—Located north of Tenjin, this area is home to Fukuoka's port and its famous fish market. While some stalls have been here for years, new yatai have recently opened, making it an exciting new spot to explore.

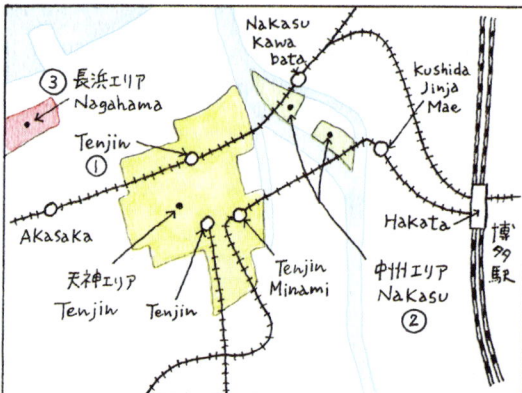

Shoyu Ramen

醤油ラーメン

屋台ラーメン
博多 豚骨ラーメン

専多 豚骨 ラーメン

ラーメン

博多屋台ばらかもん

Fukuoka's Hakata Yatai Barakamon

In this yatai located a stone's throw from the Tenjin subway station, don't miss out on their specialty: the Agodashi tonkotsu ramen. With an original broth made from flying fish, chicken carcasses and pork bones, this ramen garnished with a soft-boiled egg, chashu (pork belly), leeks and nori seaweed, has a unique flavor. The whole thing is lighter than a classic tonkotsu broth, but the combination of flying fish and the two meats gives the broth a lot of depth.

Chuo Ward, Tenjin, 2 Chome-13-1

豚骨ラーメン

Tonkotsu Ramen

TONKOTSU RAMEN

The menu at ramen yatai is usually shorter than in traditional restaurants. However, in Fukuoka, it's highly recommended to try the Tonkotsu Ramen (see recipe on p. 62)—the city's most famous culinary specialty.

TONKOTSU RAMEN

The name of this ramen from Fukuoka, on the island of Kyushu, comes from tonkotsu, which means "pork bone," the source of the savory broth. This rich and super thick soup is made by simmering pork bones, allowing the collagen and marrow to be released, giving the broth its creamy consistency.

Servings: 4 people
Preparation time: 30 min
Cooking time: 7 min + 2h 30 (for the meat and broth)

- **4 portions of dried ramen noodles (14 oz/400 g)**
- **6¾ cups (1.6 l) tonkotsu broth (see page 56)**
- **1½ lbs (700 g) chashu pork (see recipe on page 58)**
- **2 large eggs**
- **2 green onions**
- **1 sheet nori**

For the Miso Tare:
- **4 tablespoons miso paste**
- **1 tablespoon sake**
- **2 tablespoons mirin**
- **1 tablespoon soy sauce**
- **1 teaspoon grated ginger**
- **½ teaspoon toasted sesame oil**

Prepare the Miso Tare sauce by mixing all the sauce ingredients in a bowl.

Cook the eggs for 7 minutes in boiling water. Peel them and cut them in half.

Cut the chashu meat into thin slices. Finely chop the green part of the green onion. Cut the white part of the green onion into very fine julienne strips lengthwise.

Cut the nori sheet into four pieces.

Cook the noodles in a large amount of boiling water for the time indicated on the package. Drain.

In each bowl, place a little miso tare sauce, pour in the hot broth and mix. Distribute the hot noodles, then arrange the toppings on the noodles. Serve immediately.

豚骨ラーメン
Tonkotsu Ramen

TSURU-TSURU SLURPING

"Tsuru-tsuru" is a word that represents the slurping sound made when eating noodles. All Japanese slurp their noodles. It helps cool them while enhancing the flavor.

So don't hesitate to make some noise when you're sitting at the counter of a ramen stall in Japan!

SHOYU RAMEN

Soy-sauce-seasoned broth is mainly a specialty of the Tokyo region, but this version, called shoyu tare, is by far the most widespread. The restaurant Fujiya Chuka Soba, located just a short walk from Okayama Station (in western Japan, between Osaka and Hiroshima), attracts many food lovers with its rich and flavorful tonkotsu broth.

For 4 people
Preparation: 30 min
Cooking time: 5 min + 4 h for the meat and broth

- 4 portions dried ramen noodles (14 oz/400 g)
- 6¾ cups (1.6 l) tonkotsu broth (see recipe p. 56)
- ⅔ cup (150 ml) Shoyu Tare Sauce (see recipe p. 57)
- 1½ lbs (700 g) chashu meat (see recipe p. 58)
- 2½ tablespoons menma (see below)
- 1 small green onion

Cut the meat into thin slices. Finely chop the green onion, then cut the nori sheet into four pieces.

Cook the noodles in a large pot of boiling water according to the package instructions. Drain.

In each bowl, add a little tare sauce, pour in the hot broth and give it all a quick mix. Distribute the hot noodles, then arrange the toppings over the noodles.

Serve immediately.

MENMA

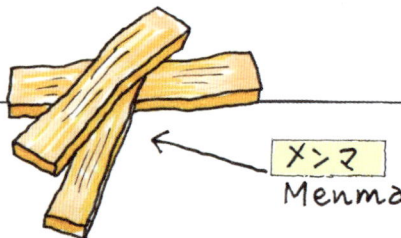

メンマ
Menma

- 1 cup (200 g) canned or bottled cooked bamboo shoots
- 1 teaspoon chicken broth
- 1 tablespoon soy sauce
- 1 tablespoon sake
- 1 tablespoon sugar
- ⅖ cup (100 ml) water

You can find these fermented bamboo shoots in Japanese grocery stores, sold in jars, but you can also easily make a non-fermented version at home.

Rinse the bamboo shoots, drain them and place them in a saucepan with the chicken broth, soy sauce, sake, sugar and water.

Cook, stirring occasionally, until the liquid has completely evaporated.

Season with a few drops of rayu (spicy sesame oil). You can store this menma in a jar in the refrigerator for up to 1 week.

Fujiya Chuka Soba Shop in Okayama

shoyu Ramen

醤油ラーメン

冨士屋メニュー
Fujiya Menu

•中華そば Chuka Soba	¥830
•チャーシュー麺 Chashu Men	¥980
•味玉中華そば Ajitama Chuka Soba	¥930
•餃子 Gyoza	¥380

Gyoza

餃子

冨士屋 MAP
Fujiya

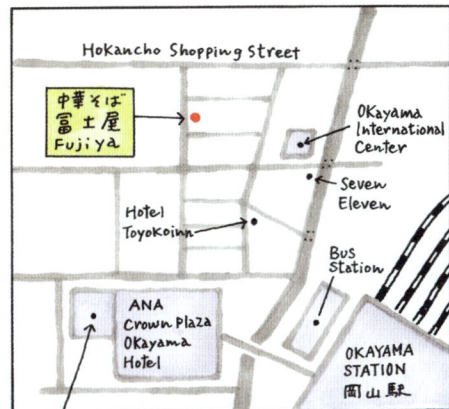

中華そば
冨士屋
Fujiya

Hokancho Shopping Street

Okayama International Center

Seven Eleven

Hotel Toyokoinn

Bus Station

ANA Crown Plaza Okayama Hotel

OKAYAMA STATION
岡山駅

Okayama Convention Center
岡山コンベンションセンター

Okayama, Kita Ward, Hokancho, 2 Chome-3-8.

Chuka Soba
Okayama Fujiya

TANTAN MEN

Tracing its origins to Sichuan, this Japanese version will delight spice lovers with its chili-infused broth—both bold and creamy, due to the sesame paste.

**For 4 people
Preparation: 20 min
Cooking time: 15 min**

- 12 oz (360 g) dried ramen noodles
- 4 cups (1 l) chicken broth (or ramen broth, p. 56)
- 1⅔ cups (400 ml) soy milk
- 4 tablespoons sesame paste
- 4 tablespoons soy sauce
- 1 tablespoon rayu (spicy chili oil)

For the topping:

- 14 oz (400 g) ground pork
- ½ cup (60 g) shelled edamame (soybeans, can be replaced with fava beans)
- ¾ inch (2 cm) fresh ginger, grated
- 2 garlic cloves, grated
- ½ tablespoon gochujang (spicy Korean bean paste)
- 2 tablespoons soy sauce
- 1 teaspoon rice vinegar
- 1 tablespoon sunflower oil
- 1 green onion, chopped
- 1 handful daikon radish sprouts (optional, available in organic food stores)

Cook the edamame according to the package instructions (3 to 4 minutes) in a pot of boiling water. Drain and set aside.

In a wok, heat the sunflower oil over high heat, then stir-fry the ground pork for 2 minutes without stopping. Add the ginger and garlic, and continue to stir-fry for another 2 minutes. Then, add the chili paste, soy sauce and vinegar. Mix everything well and then cook for another 2 minutes.

In a saucepan, bring the chicken broth and soy milk to a simmer. In a bowl, mix the sesame paste, soy sauce and chili oil. Thin the mixture with a small amount of broth, then incorporate it into the saucepan. Keep warm.

Cook the noodles in a pot of boiling water according to the package instructions (2 to 3 minutes). Drain the noodles and divide them into 4 large bowls. Pour the hot spicy broth over the noodles, then add the pork mixture and edamame.

Sprinkle with chopped green onions and enjoy immediately.

ラー油

RAYU

Also known as "layu," this spicy sesame oil originates from China. It can be found on the counter of every ramen restaurant. Just a few drops are enough to enhance ramen noodles and gyoza.

HOMEMADE CHILI OIL (RAYU SUBSTITUTE)

In a saucepan, heat ⅔ cup (150 ml) sunflower oil and ⅖ cup (100 ml) toasted sesame oil over low heat. Add: 2 green onions, roughly chopped, 3 garlic cloves, crushed, 1½ inches (4 cm) fresh ginger, sliced, 1 teaspoon coriander seeds, 2 star anise and a cinnamon stick. Let it infuse over very low heat for 15 minutes. Place 3 tablespoons (40 g) chili flakes in a jar, then pour the hot infused oil over them while straining out the solids. Mix and let cool. This oil can be stored for several months in the refrigerator.

CUP NOODLES

Ramen experienced a huge boom with the invention of Japanese instant noodles, known throughout Asia now as cup noodles.

Cup Noodle
カップヌードル

歴史
THE HISTORY

In 1958, Momofuku Ando invented instant noodles. After months of searching for a way to preserve and quickly prepare ramen, he had the idea—while watching his wife prepare tempura—to fry the noodles, cooking and dehydrating them at the same time. This method allowed them to be prepared quickly by simply rehydrating them with hot water. Instant noodles were then marketed and immediately gained a large audience.

A few years later, during a trip to the United States, Momofuku Ando noticed Americans crushing blocks of instant noodles into mugs before pouring in boiling water. This gave him the idea to sell them directly in disposable cups. This was the birth of the first cup noodles!

カップヌードルの種類
CUP NOODLE VARIETIES

Since the creation of the first chicken broth cup noodles, many other varieties have emerged, not only in Japan but also worldwide, adapting to the tastes of different markets. For example, in Korea and Southeast Asia, spicier versions are found.

The main flavors include chicken, beef and seafood, but curry-flavored noodles have also gained immense popularity.

カップヌードルを作る3つのステップ

PREPARING CUP NOODLES IN 3 STEPS

2. Close the cup and let it sit for 3 minutes.

1. Open the cup lid partially (without removing it completely) and pour in boiling water until the noodles are fully covered (a visible line indicates the correct level).

3. Enjoy them hot using chopsticks!

カップラーメン自販機

NOODLE VENDING MACHINES

In Japan, instant noodles are sold in supermarkets and konbini (convenience stores) that are open 24 hours a day (see p. 160). Additionally, there are many vending machines, similar to drink dispensers (see p. 192), allowing people to grab a meal at any time of the day or night.

Here's a small guide to buying your instant ramen on the street!

Six available varieties, including 2 udon options

Button to dispense hot water

Compartment to place the opened noodle cup

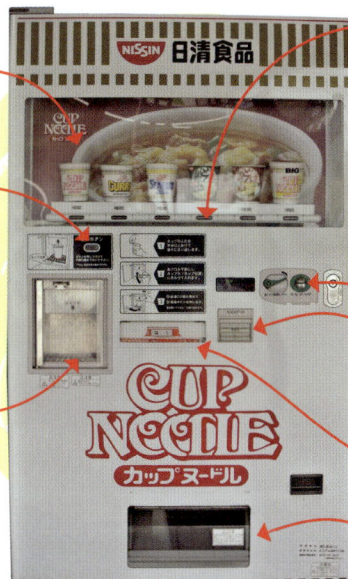

How to use the machine:

1. Insert money and select the noodles you want.

2. Remove the cup and open the lid.

3. Place the open cup in the water dispensing compartment.

4. Press the button to add hot water.

5. Remove the cup, cover the lid and let it sit for 1–2 minutes.

Slots to insert bills or coins

Chopsticks available

Noodle dispenser

SHOYU RAMEN & DEMI KATSUDON

Date Soba, a ramen restaurant founded in 1955, is a favorite of Takashi Fujii, who illustrated this book. He's spent many years exploring the streets of his hometown, Okayama, in search of hidden, unassuming places that one might otherwise pass by without a second glance.

SHOYU RAMEN WITH CHICKEN BROTH

See the recipe on p. 64, using chicken broth (p. 56) instead of tonkotsu broth.

デミカツ丼 DEMI KATSUDON

The specialty of this restaurant is one of Okayama's signature dishes: Demi Katsudon. This dish, influenced by Western cuisine, consists of tonkatsu (see p. 110) served over a bowl of rice, topped with finely sliced and blanched cabbage, then drizzled with demi-glace (a reduced veal stock). It's served alongside ramen, either as a main dish or a side dish.

For 4 people
Preparation Time: 20 min
Cooking Time: 1 hr 30 min

- **4 tonkatsu fried pork cutlets (see p. 110)**
- **4 fresh egg yolks**

For about 2 cups (½ l) of Demi-Glace:
- **1 medium onion, quartered**
- **½ medium carrot, quartered**
- **1 bouquet garni (bundled herbs, typically bay leaves and fresh parsley and thyme)**
- **5 cups (1.2 l) beef broth**
- **1½ tablespoons butter**
- **¼ cup (30 g) flour**
- **A drizzle of olive oil**
- **Salt and pepper, to taste**

Prepare the tonkatsu by following the recipe on page 110.

Then prepare the Demi-Glace. Place the vegetables and the bouquet garni in a large pot, seasoning generously with salt and pepper. Sauté the vegetables, with a drizzle of olive oil, for about 10 minutes, stirring occasionally. Pour in the broth, bring to a boil, skimming off any impurities, and let it simmer over low heat for 1 hour 15 minutes. Remove the bouquet garni, blend the contents of the pot and then strain.

Prepare the roux. Melt the butter in a saucepan, add the flour, whisking continuously until the mixture just begins to brown. Add the strained broth and let it thicken over low heat. Adjust the seasoning, if needed.

Place the freshly cooked and sliced tonkatsu pieces in bowls of steaming hot rice. Generously drizzle with the Demi-Glace. Place an egg yolk in the center of the bowl and serve immediately.

Date Soba Shop in Okayama

Shoyu Ramen

醤油ラーメン

Demi Katsudon

デミカツ丼

だてそば

Date Soba

だてそば メニュー
Date Soba Menu

● 支那そば	———	¥750
Shina Soba	大 Big (¥900)	
● かつ丼	———	¥950
Katsudon	大 Big (¥1.200)	
● そば定食 (そばと小かつ丼)		
Soba Set	———	¥1.500
● かつ丼定食 (かつ丼と小そば)		
Katsudon Set	———	¥1.600

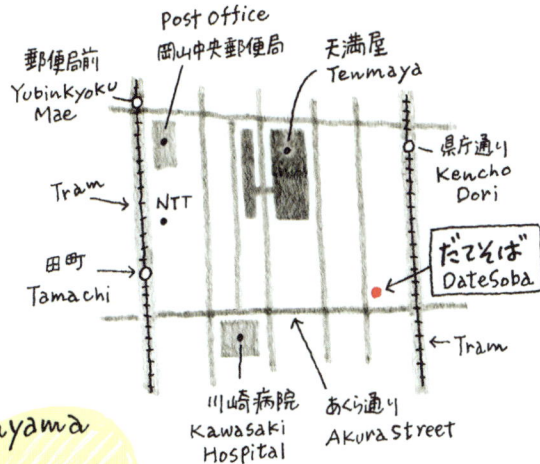

Post Office
岡山中央郵便局

郵便局前
Yubinkyoku
Mae

天満屋
Tenmaya

Tram

NTT

県庁通り
Kencho
Dori

田町
Tamachi

だてそば
Date Soba

← Tram

川崎病院
Kawasaki
Hospital

あくら通り
Akura Street

Okayama
Date Soba
MAP

**Okayama, Kita Ward,
Omotecho, 2 Chome-3-60**

GYOZA DUMPLINGS

These dumplings are crispy and crunchy on the bottom and soft and chewy on top, giving them a unique texture. The result is simply addictive!

For 20 gyoza
Preparation: 30 min
Cooking: 10 to 15 min

- **20 fresh or frozen gyoza wrappers**

For the Filling:
- **4 oz (120 g) minced pork**
- **8 to 10 cabbage leaves (4oz/120 g), thinly sliced**
- **1 spring onion, finely chopped**
- **1 clove garlic, minced**
- **1 teaspoon fresh ginger, grated**
- **3 tablespoons soy sauce**
- **3 teaspoons sesame oil, plus a drizzle for cooking**
- **Salt and freshly ground pepper**

For the Dipping Sauce:
- **2 tablespoons rice vinegar**
- **2 tablespoons soy sauce**
- **Fresh ginger, shredded**

Prepare the Filling by blanching the cabbage leaves for 1 minute in a pot of boiling water, then drain them and finely chop them. In a bowl, mix all the filling ingredients together.

Place a generous teaspoon of filling in the center of each wrapper, moisten the edge of the upper half of the wrapper and fold it in half, ensuring as little air as possible is trapped inside.

Seal the edges, then pleat them to securely close the gyoza. Heat a drizzle of oil in a pan over medium heat and brown the gyoza for 5 minutes on one side.

Pour in water to cover the dumplings halfway, then cover and cook over high heat until the water has completely evaporated. Remove the lid and continue cooking for 1 more minute.

Meanwhile, prepare the Dipping Sauce by mixing the rice vinegar and soy sauce and adding the ginger. Place the gyoza on a plate, turning them over to display the golden side. Enjoy with the Dipping Sauce.

NOTE

To achieve a beautiful lacy effect on your gyoza, add a mixture of water and potato or cornstarch to the pan or griddle right at the end of the cooking process.

Preparing the gyoza

SHISO DAIKON OROSHI GYOZA

This restaurant, specializing in gyoza, is located in the lively Yukakucho district, just a few steps from Tokyo Station and the Imperial Palace. The extensive menu offers the chance to discover many variations (see p. 74), such as curry or cheese gyoza. Even those with a sweet tooth can enjoy crispy chocolate gyoza, served with a scoop of vanilla ice cream!

For 24 gyoza
Preparation: 30 min
Cooking: 10 to 15 min

- **24 gyoza wrappers (available in the frozen section of Asian grocery stores)**

For the Filling:
- **¼ lb (120 g) boneless chicken**
- **6 to 8 Napa cabbage leaves**
- **2 dried shiitake mushrooms**
- **1 green onion**
- **1 clove garlic, minced**
- **1 teaspoon ginger, grated**
- **3 tablespoons soy sauce**
- **2 tablespoons toasted sesame oil, plus extra for cooking**
- **Salt and freshly ground pepper, to taste**

For serving:
- **⅔ cup (100 g) daikon, grated**
- **4 shiso leaves (or basil leaves)**
- **2 tablespoons lemon juice**
- **2 tablespoons soy sauce**

Prepare the Filling:

Soak the dried shiitake mushrooms in a bowl of water for 15 minutes. Drain them well, squeezing out the excess water with your hands. Remove the stems and finely chop the mushrooms. Blanch the cabbage leaves in a pot of boiling water for 1 minute, then drain and finely chop them. In a bowl, mix all the filling ingredients.

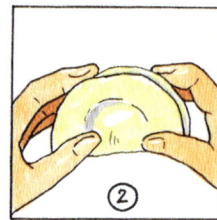

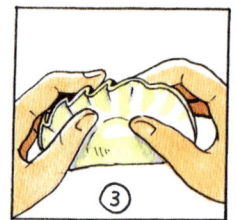

Place a heaping teaspoon of Filling in the center of each gyoza wrapper. Moisten the edge of the upper half of the wrapper and fold it in half, making sure to enclose as little air as possible inside the dumpling. Press the edges together, then pleat them to properly seal the gyoza.

Heat a drizzle of oil in a pan over medium, then brown the gyoza for 5 minutes on one side. Pour water up to half the height of the gyoza, cover and then cook on high heat until all the water has evaporated.

Prepare the Garnishes:

Grate the peeled daikon using a fine grater. Chop the shiso leaves. Mix the lemon juice and soy sauce. Remove the lid and continue cooking for 1 minute.

Place the gyoza on a plate with the golden side facing up. Garnish with grated daikon and shiso. Drizzle with a little sauce before serving.

NOTICE

GADO-SHITA

Many small eateries or izakaya can be found along the Yamanote train line. These charmingly old-fashioned spots, called gado-shita (or "under the beams"), are nestled beneath the brick arches of the railway line. The atmosphere is authentic and lively, especially on weekday evenings when office workers from nearby business districts come to relax over drinks and small bites.

Chao Chao Gyoza Shop in Yurakucho

浪花ひとくち餃子 餃子 チャオ チャオ 々

浪花ひとくち餃子 チャオチャオ

OPEN

名物

Shisodaikon Oroshi Gyoza

しそ大根おろし餃子

チャオチャオ餃子
Chao Chao Gyoza

アイスクリーム チョコレート餃子
Ice Creem Chocolate Gyoza

Chao Chao Gyoza Menu

- チャオチャオ餃子 (2枚) ¥670
  ChaoChao Gyoza
- プリプリ海老餃子 (3コ) ¥420
  Puri Puri Ebi Gyoza
- 鶏チーズ餃子 (3コ) ¥350
  Tori cheese Gyoza
- 梅シソ餃子 (3コ) ¥300
  Ume shiso Gyoza
- 水餃子 (3コ) ¥350
  Sui Gyoza

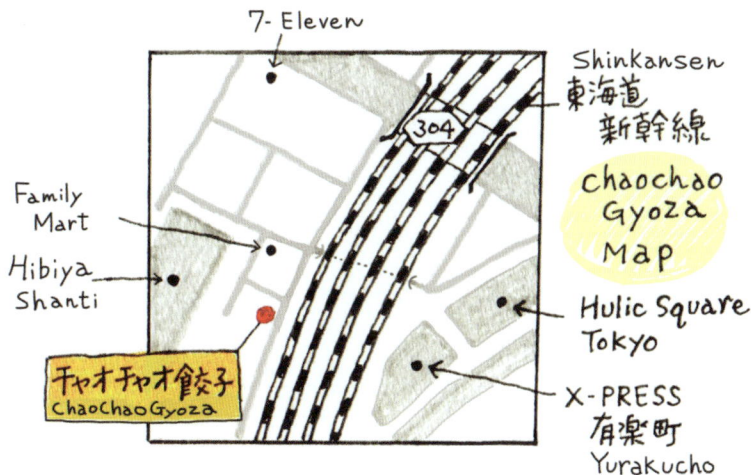

7-Eleven

Shinkansen
東海道
新幹線

304

chaochao
Gyoza
Map

Family
Mart

Hibiya
Shanti

Hulic Square
Tokyo

X-PRESS
有楽町
Yurakucho

チャオチャオ餃子
ChaoChao Gyoza

Tokyo, Chiyoda-ku, Yurakucho
1-chome, 2-9

OYAKI BUNS

These stuffed buns are a specialty of Nagano Prefecture. They can be made in a savory version with different types of vegetables (eggplant, squash and spinach are popular) or in a sweet version with anko, or red bean paste.

For 8 oyaki
Preparation: 25 min
Dough resting time: 30 min
Cooking: 25 min

- **¾ cup (100 g) white flour**
- **¾ cup (100 g) rice flour**
- **½ teaspoon salt**

For the Filling:
- **2½ cups (600 g) eggplant**
- **2 level tablespoons white miso**
- **2 tablespoons sake**
- **1 tablespoon granulated sugar**
- **1 tablespoon sunflower oil**
- **½ tablespoon toasted sesame oil**

Sift both types of flour and the salt into a bowl. Add ½ cup (120 ml) of water and mix by hand to obtain a smooth, soft dough. Let it rest for 30 minutes under a damp cloth.

Divide the dough into 8 pieces. Roll each piece out with a rolling pin into discs about 3 inches (8 cm) in diameter.

Prepare the Filling:

In a bowl, mix the miso, sake, and sugar. Cut the eggplants into small cubes, then sauté them in a pan with a drizzle of sunflower oil for about 5 minutes, stirring regularly. Lower the heat, add the miso mixture, and continue cooking for 2 more minutes.

Prepare the Oyaki:

Place 2 tablespoons of Filling in the center of each dough disc. Close it to form a pouch, folding the edges inward to create a ball (and removing any excess dough).

Heat the sesame oil in a pan over medium and brown the Oyaki for about 6 minutes, turning them regularly. Once they've taken on a nice golden color, pour in just less than ¼ cup (50 ml) of water, then cover and cook on high heat until all the water has evaporated.

Remove the lid and continue cooking for another 4 minutes, turning the buns two or three times.

TIP
For a spicier flavor, add a generous pinch of shichimi togarashi, a blend of seven spices that can be easily found in Asian grocery stores. If unavailable, use a pinch of chili powder instead.

YOKOCHO SIDE LANES

These hidden alleyways (yokocho means "the alley next door") transport tourists to an authentic Japan, where smoky food stalls share space with old-fashioned izakaya. Here is a glimpse of a few yokocho worth discovering.

思い出横丁

OMOIDE YOKOCHO

Just a few steps west of Tokyo's bustling Shinjuku Station, an evening stroll here will reveal a different side of this district, one of the busiest in the capital.

Subway : Shinjuku

有楽町 ガード下

YURAKUCHO

Most of these places have indeed developed beneath the elevated railway lines of the capital. Near Yurakucho Station, you'll find numerous izakaya where you can sit down for a meal. The sound of passing trains is part of the charm of the place!

Subway : Yurakucho

産直 横丁

SANCHOKU YOKOCHO

Hidden under the tracks of Japan Rail, finding the entrance to this yokocho located beneath a bridge won't be easy. But once you step into this alley, you'll be transported to a nostalgic atmosphere with its many small shops and lanterns.

Subway : Yurakucho

法善寺横丁

YOZENJI YOKOCHO

In the heart of the lively Dotombori district in Osaka, these two alleys take you back to the Edo period of Japan. More upscale than the popular yokocho of Tokyo, the restaurants here offer traditional and refined cuisine. This timeless visit ends at the Hōzen-ji Temple.

🚇 **Subway** : Namba

NIKUMAN BUNS

These delicious steamed meat buns originated in China but were quickly adopted by the Japanese, who even created a sweet version filled with anko.

For 8 buns
Preparation: 40 min
Resting time: 50 min
Cooking time: 15 min

For the Dough:
- 1¾ cups (275 g) flour, plus extra for kneading
- 1⅔ tablespoons sugar
- 1 teaspoon dry yeast
- 1 teaspoon baking powder
- ½ teaspoon salt
- 1 tablespoon vegetable oil
- ⅔ cup (150 ml) warm water

For the Filling:
- 2 dried shiitake mushrooms
- ½ lb (225 g) ground pork
- ½ onion, finely chopped
- 1 teaspoon grated ginger
- ½ tablespoon soy sauce
- ½ tablespoon miso
- ½ tablespoon toasted sesame oil
- ½ tablespoon potato starch or cornstarch
- Freshly ground black pepper, to taste

Start by rehydrating the shiitake mushrooms in a small bowl of water for 20 minutes.

Prepare the Dough:

In a bowl, mix the flour, sugar, both types of yeast and the salt. Add the oil, mix and then gradually incorporate the water until you get a soft Dough.

Lightly flour the work surface and knead the Dough for about 10 minutes.

Form a ball, place it in a bowl, cover it with a cloth and let it double in volume in a warm, draft-free place for at least 30 minutes.

Prepare the Filling:

Drain the rehydrated shiitake mushrooms, squeezing them well in your hands. Remove the stems and finely chop them. In a mixing bowl, combine all the Filling ingredients.

Shape the Buns:

Take the Dough and, on a floured work surface, form a cylinder. Cut it into 8 equal parts, then roll out each piece into a circle about 4 inches (10 cm) in diameter.

Place a heaping tablespoon of Filling in the center of each Dough circle and seal each.

Place the buns on a square of parchment paper inside a steamer basket, spacing them out as they will expand.

Heat water in the pot that will hold the steamer basket without bringing it to a boil. Turn off the heat, place the steamer basket over the pot and let the buns rise for 20 minutes.

Steam the nikuman for 15 minutes.

Shaping the nikuman

TACHIGUI STANDS

In Japan, many popular dishes such as soba (p. 88), tonkatsu (p. 110) and donburi (p. 134) can be eaten quickly on the go or while waiting for a train. These restaurants, called tachigui, are located in busy areas such as train stations or shopping centers and are essentially the Japanese version of fast food. Orders are placed through an automated machine where you insert money, press a button to select what you want and receive a ticket.

ANY TIME OF THE DAY

These places aren't just busy around mealtimes, but from early morning, office workers grab a bowl of noodles before heading to the office. These eateries remain bustling throughout the day, though peak hours are naturally during lunch and after work.

HOW THE ORDER MACHINE WORKS

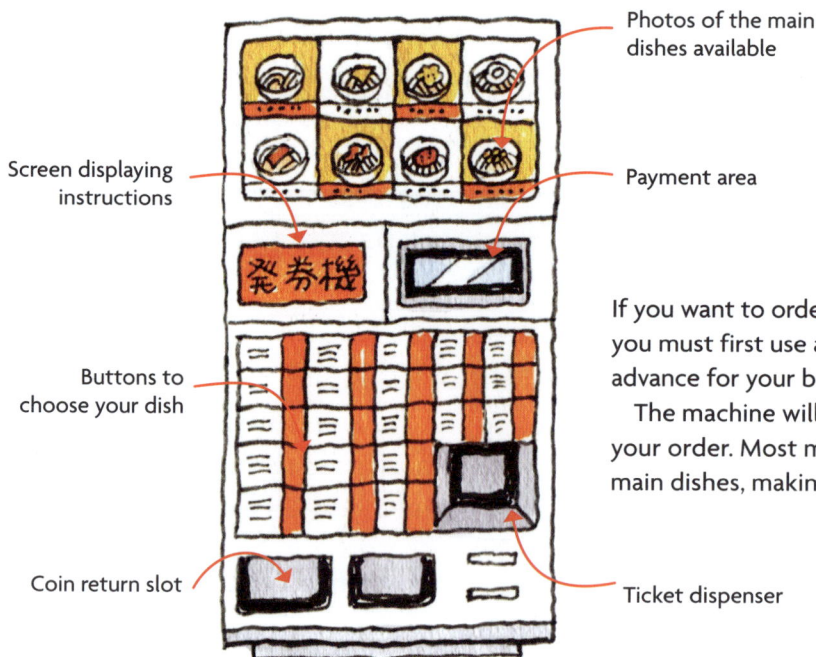

Photos of the main dishes available

Screen displaying instructions

Payment area

発券機

Buttons to choose your dish

If you want to order at this type of restaurant, you must first use an automatic machine to pay in advance for your bowl of noodles.

The machine will give you a ticket, which initiates your order. Most machines display photos of the main dishes, making ordering much easier!

Coin return slot

Ticket dispenser

TYPES OF TACHIGUI

The most common tachigui are tachigui soba, offering soba and udon noodles. These are often chain restaurants located inside train stations or directly on the platform. However, some small, independent, family-run shops still preserve the post-war Japanese atmosphere, when this type of fast dining expanded rapidly alongside urbanization.

Beyond noodles, you can also find tachigui sushi spots and, most notably, bars or izakaya (places where people drink while sharing dishes), commonly referred to as a standing bar (p. 202).

POPULAR DISHES

Most tachigui soba serve both soba and udon at very affordable prices. Here are some of the most common dishes:

KAKE SOBA: (see p. 92 for the udon version)

KITSUNE SOBA: (p. 90)

TEMPURA SOBA: (p. 88)

ZARU SOBA: (cold noodles served with tsuyu sauce)

立ち食いそば
Tachigui Soba

RECOMMENDED PLACES IN TOKYO

Toyoshima Iidabashi

For a more traditional experience, check out this soba restaurant, located just a short walk from Iidabashi Station in Tokyo. You'll likely see a steady stream of office workers during their lunch break, but this restaurant stays busy all day, and many people make a special stop just to enjoy a bowl of soba.

Esoragoto Udon

This charming udon restaurant is located in the trendy Harajuku district of Tokyo. It's not a typical tachigui, as not only is the quality of the rice flour-based noodles exceptional, but the minimalist decor is also carefully designed. So a visit is essential for all udon lovers!

TEMPURA SOBA

Soba means "buckwheat" in Japanese. These noodles are made with whole-meal buckwheat flour, sometimes with a small amount of wheat flour added to bind the dough. Their often simple preparation has made soba noodles synonymous with quick and healthy cuisine.

Serves: 4
Preparation: 20 min
Cooking: 25 min

- ¾ lb (350 g) dried soba noodles
- 1 green onion, chopped
- 8 medium tempura shrimp (see p. 113)

For the Broth:
- 6 cups (1.5 l) dashi broth (available in Asian grocery stores or make your own, see the Note)
- 4 tablespoons soy sauce
- 4 tablespoons mirin
- 2 tablespoons sake
- 1 teaspoon salt

First, prepare the tempura shrimp by following the recipe on page 113.

Prepare the Broth:

Bring all the Broth ingredients to a boil. Let it boil for 1 minute and keep warm.

Prepare the Noodles:

Cook the soba noodles in a pot of boiling water according to the package instructions (4 to 5 minutes). Drain the noodles and divide them into 4 large bowls. Add the hot tempura shrimp. Pour the steaming Broth over the top.

Garnish with chopped spring onions and serve immediately.

NOTE

Make Your Own Dashi Broth: In a saucepan, bring 6 cups (1.5 l) of water to a boil with a piece of kombu seaweed. Let it boil for 5 minutes, then remove the seaweed. Remove from the heat, then add a large handful of katsuobushi dried bonito flakes. When all the flakes settle to the bottom of the pot, strain the broth.

TIP
This recipe works well with many types of tempura: mushrooms, onions, fish, eggplant. Feel free to adjust based on the season!

KITSUNE SOBA

Soba noodles are always prepared simply in order to enhance the hearty flavor of the noodles. In summer, they're enjoyed cold, simply dipped in a tsuyu sauce. However, they're most often served hot in a broth, as in this versionwith fried abura-age tofu.

Serves: 4
Preparation: 15 min
Cooking: 12 min

- 9 oz (250 g) dried soba noodles
- 2 pieces of abura-age (available in frozen section of Asian grocery stores)
- 5 cups (1.2 l) dashi broth (available in Asian grocery stores or see recipe on p. 88)
- 2 green onions, chopped

For the Tsuyu Sauce:
- 1 piece kombu seaweed (about 4 inches/10 cm square)
- 2 dried shiitake mushrooms
- 4 tablespoons soy sauce
- 4 tablespoons mirin
- 2 tablespoons sake
- ¾ cup (180 ml) water

Prepare the Tsuyu Sauce:

Place the kombu, shiitake mushrooms, soy sauce, mirin, sake and water in a saucepan over medium heat. Once it reaches a boil, turn off the heat and let it cool. Strain the sauce.

Prepare the Inari-Age:

Place the pieces of fried tofu (abura-age) in a strainer. Pour boiling water over them to remove some of the oil. Drain well.

Cut each abura-age diagonally into four pieces to form triangles.

Place the triangles in a saucepan with the Tsuyu Sauce. Cover, bring to a boil and then cook for 3 minutes. To finish, add the dashi broth and bring to a boil again.

Prepare the Noodles:

Cook the soba noodles in a pot of boiling water according to the package instructions (4 to 5 minutes). Drain them thoroughly.

Divide the noodles into 4 large bowls. Pour the hot broth over them, then add the abura-age triangles and the chopped spring onions.

Enjoy while hot!

油揚げ

ABURA-AGE

These fried tofu pouches are made by deep-frying thin slices of firm tofu in two oil baths: a first fry at a low temperature (around 250°F/120°C) to make the tofu puff up, and a second fry at 390°F/200°C to give it color. They're mainly used to make inarizushi (fried tofu pouches stuffed with vinegared rice).

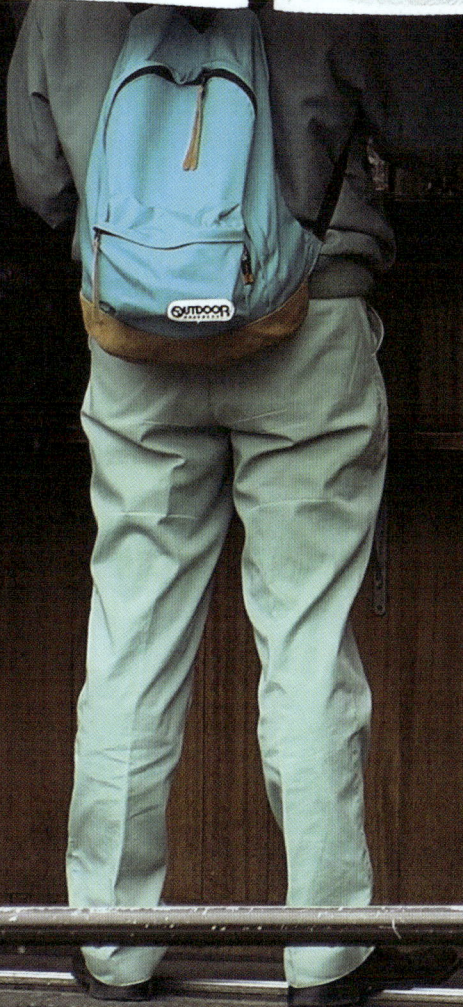

KARE UDON

Kare is derived from the Japanese pronunciation of "curry." Kare rice, a Japanese-style curry served with rice, has exploded in popularity in recent years. This udon noodle version is available on the menu at most tachigui soba restaurants (see pages 86–87).

Serves 4
Preparation: 20 min
Cooking: 35 min

- 1¾ lbs (800 g) fresh udon noodles (or 12 oz/350 g dried udon)
- 2 chicken thighs (½ lb/225 g total)
- 1 small carrot
- 1 baby leek or large green onion
- 1 small garlic clove
- ½ cup (100 g) Japanese curry (see the Tip below)
- Sunflower oil, to drizzle

Debone the chicken thighs and remove the skin.

Cut the meat into cubes. Peel the carrot and slice it into rounds. Wash the leek and cut it into ¾-inch (2-cm) pieces. Peel and chop the garlic.

Heat the sunflower oil in a saucepan over high heat, then sauté the garlic, carrot and leek for 3 to 4 minutes. Add the chicken cubes and brown them, stirring occasionally.

Pour in 4 cups (1 l) of water, bring to a boil, then let it simmer over low heat for 15 minutes.

Crumble the curry into the mixture and stir to dissolve. Let it simmer for 5 minutes, stirring occasionally until the sauce thickens.

Cook the noodles in a pot of boiling water according to the package instructions—about 2 to 4 minutes (or 5 minutes for dried noodles).

Drain the noodles and divide them among 4 bowls. Pour the curry mixture over the top and serve immediately.

TIP
Japanese curry comes in tablet form, which you break apart and dissolve into the dish. There are different levels of spiciness depending on the name: amakuchi (mild), chukuchi (medium-spicy) or karakuchi (spicy).

KAKE UDON

Udon, along with soba and ramen, are the most common noodles in Japan. They're mainly served in a broth with a simple topping (as in this recipe), in a nabe (or hot pot) or cold with tsuyu sauce.

For 4 people
Preparation: 15 min
Cooking: 12 min

- ¾ lb (350 g) dried udon noodles
- 1 green onion
- 1 tablespoon dried wakame seaweed
- 4 tablespoons tenkasu (tempura flakes, see Tip below)

For the Broth:
- 5 cups (1.2 l) dashi broth (available in Asian grocery stores or see p. 88)
- 4 tablespoons soy sauce
- 4 tablespoons mirin
- 1 tablespoon sugar
- 1 teaspoon salt

Rehydrate the dried wakame seaweed in a bowl of cold water for 5 minutes. Drain well, squeezing out excess water with your hands.

Prepare the Broth:

Bring all the Broth ingredients to a boil. Let it boil for 1 minute and keep warm.

Prepare the Noodles:

Cook the udon noodles in a pot of boiling water according to the package instructions (4 to 5 minutes). Drain the noodles and divide them into 4 large bowls. Pour the hot Broth over them and add the toppings (tenkasu, wakame, green onion). Serve immediately.

TenKasu
天かず
Tempura Flakes

Negi
ネギ
Green Onion

WaKame
ワカメ
Seaweed

TIP
TENKASU: These tempura flakes are used to top many noodle dishes (soba and udon) and add flavor and crunch to certain dishes like takoyaki or okonomiyaki. You can find them ready-to-use in Asian grocery stores, or you can easily make them at home by frying dollops of tempura batter (see p. 112) in oil.

Udon Kameya Shop in Okayama

Udon Kameya
うどん かめや

Onigiri
おにぎり

Nasutenpura
なすの天ぷら

A rice ball (see p. 120) and eggplant tempura (see p. 113)

かけうどん
Kake Udon

Udon Kameya Menu

- かけうどん ...... (1玉)¥320
  Kake Udon (2玉)¥420
- ざるうどん (S)¥500
  Zaru Udon (L)¥600
- たらいうどん ...... (S)¥520
  Tarai Udon (L)¥620
- 温玉ぶっかけうどん (S)¥620
  Ontama Bukkake (L)¥720
- 鍋焼きうどん ¥900
  Nabeyaki Udon
- ※Dinner Time Only

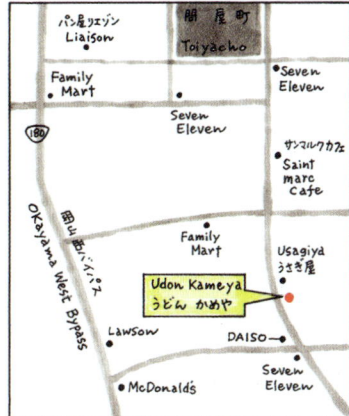

パン屋リエゾン
Liaison

朋屋町
Toiyacho

Family
Mart

Seven
Eleven

Seven
Eleven

サンマルクカフェ
Saint
marc
Cafe

180

Okayama West Bypass
岡山西バイパス

Family
Mart

Usagiya
うさぎ屋

Udon Kameya
うどん かめや

Lawson

DAISO

McDonald's

Seven
Eleven

Okayama, Kita Ward, Ima,
8 Chome-16-33

95

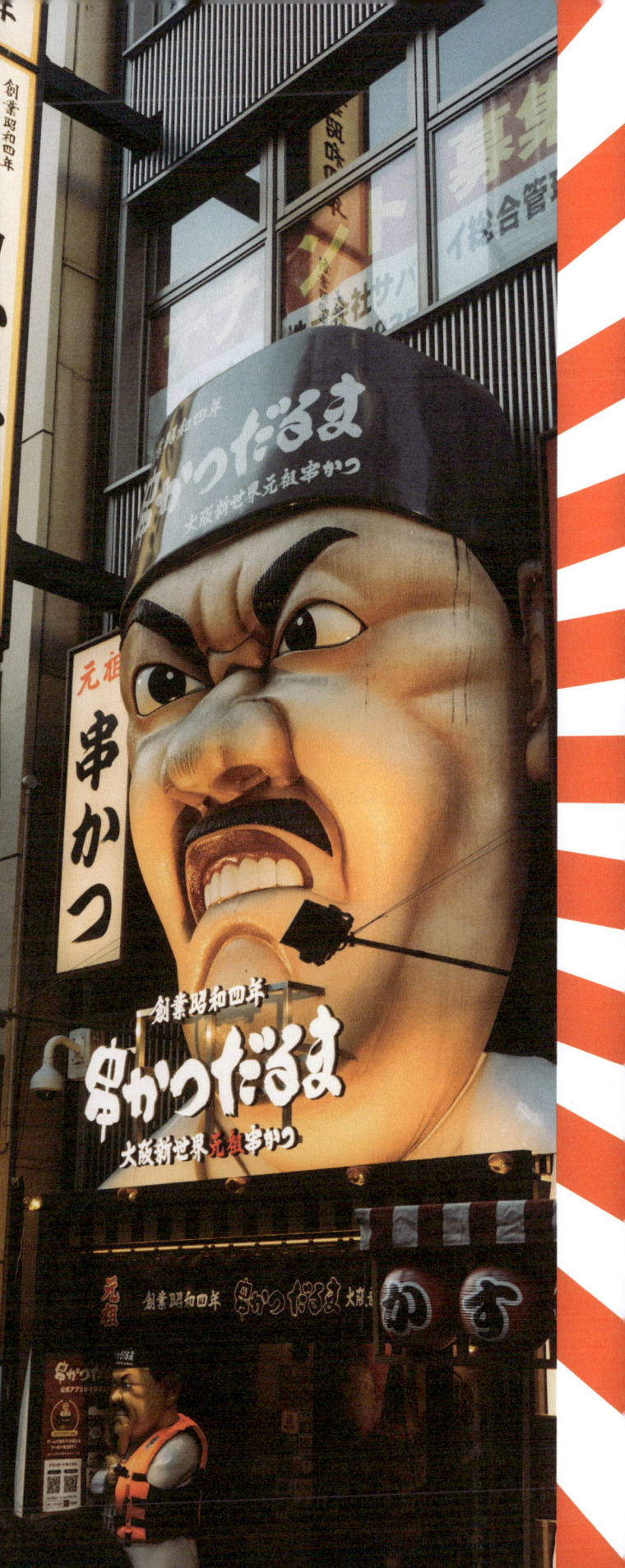

THE RULES FOR GOOD FRYING

Japanese street food offers a range of deep-fried delicacies (tempura, korokke, karaage and tonkatsu, for starters). Whatever dish you're preparing, here are a few tips in order to do it properly.

Coatings

There are three main types of coating:

TEMPURA PASTE: see the recipe opposite, used for tempura doughnuts (p. 113) and to make tonkastu (p. 110).

PANKO: breadcrumbs with an extra crunchy texture, for korokke (p. 100), tonkatsu (p. 110) and kushikatsu (p. 114).

POTATO FLOUR: katakuriko in Japanese, used for karaage (p. 116).

Panko-style breadcrumbs

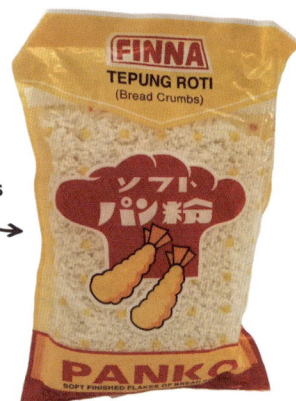

The Oil

CHOOSE THE RIGHT OIL: Use a neutral oil that can be heated to a high temperature (sunflower or peanut).

THE RIGHT TEMPERATURE IS 340°F/170°C: The oil must never smoke, a sure indicator that it's become too hot.

USE THE RIGHT QUANTITY OF OIL: You need enough oil to completely immerse the food for even cooking.

DURING COOKING: Use a skimmer to remove any small bits that may burn and spoil the taste.

TO REUSE YOUR OIL: Once the cooking is done and the oil has cooled, filter it and store it in a closed jar away from light.

The Secrets to Making Successful Tempura

ICE WATER: Tempura is light and crispy due to the contrast between the cold batter and the hot oil, which creates a thermal shock. So use ice-cold water to make the batter, and use it immediately (or refrigerate it).

DON'T OVERMIX: Don't stir the batter too long which will make the coating too elastic. It's okay if the batter is lumpy.

USE CHOPSTICKS: Use chopsticks rather than a whisk to mix it. The batter doesn't have to be smooth, it can contain lumps.

THE RIGHT TEMPERATURE: Check that the oil has reached the proper temperature by dipping the end of your wooden chopsticks into it. If bubbles rise to the surface, it's ready! The ideal temperature is 340°F (170°C), and it's important to maintain this temperature throughout the frying process.

THE RIGHT POT: Make sure the pot is wide and deep enough to hold the right amount of oil and that the ingredients are not too tightly packed together when frying them, as they will stick together.

DRAIN WELL: This step is essential to avoid greasy tempura. For a crispier result, use a stainless-steel drip pan rather than paper towels.

TEMPURA BATTER

If you can find it, use tempura flour, which has starch and baking soda premixed in it. It's sold in Asian grocery stores. Or use the recipe below to make you own.

In a bowl, quickly beat 1 cold egg with chopsticks. Add ⅞ cup (200 ml) ice-cold water. Then add ¾ cup (110 g) wheat flour and 1 tablespoon (10 g) potato starch to the bowl, sifted beforehand, and mix.

PRO TIP

DOUBLE FRYING

To obtain a perfect crisp, try cooking the ingredients twice. First, fry in oil at 320° F (160° C) until lightly colored, then after draining for 5 minutes, return to slightly hotter oil at 355° F (180° C) for a second frying, to obtain a golden color and perfectly crunchy exterior.

KOROKKE

Korokke are delicious croquettes, usually made with potatoes and meat, coated in panko breadcrumbs and deep-fried to a golden brown for an irresistibly crispy texture. Pop one in your mouth, then pop another!

For 6 croquettes
Preparation: 20 min
Cooking time: 40 min

- ½ lb (225 g) ground beef
- 6 medium potatoes (2 lbs/ 900 g total)
- 2 large eggs
- 1 medium onion
- 1 medium carrot
- 2 tablespoons potato starch
- 3 tablespoons panko breadcrumbs
- Sunflower oil, to fry
- Tonkatsu sauce, to serve
- Salt and pepper, to taste

Cook the potatoes in a pot of salted boiling water for about 20 minutes. Drain and peel them, then mash them with a fork in a bowl.

Separate the egg whites from the yolks. In a pan, heat a little sunflower oil over medium and sauté the chopped onion and carrot for about 3 minutes. Add the ground beef, season with salt and cook over high heat for 4 to 5 minutes.

Incorporate the mixture into the mashed potatoes and mix well. Remove from heat and stir in the egg yolks while mixing. Season again with salt and pepper.

Shape the mixture into 6 balls.

Beat the egg whites in a bowl. Place the potato starch on one plate and the panko breadcrumbs on another. Coat each ball in potato starch, then in the beaten egg whites and finally in the panko breadcrumbs.

Heat the oil in a wok and fry the croquettes for about 5 minutes, until they're golden brown.

Drain the croquettes on paper towels and serve them with tonkatsu sauce.

TIP
You can also use other vegetables like mushrooms or broccoli instead of or in addition to carrots. A vegetarian version with a mix of mushrooms can be just as delicious!

ぐち唐揚
京都ではば甘鯛とぐちと言ってます
一本
240円

じゃがいも玉葱がおいしい牛肉コロッケ
井上の
王様コロッケ
京錦路 井上
一ケ
200円
税込

とってもやわらかな美味しさ
ひれカツ
豚串
京錦路 井上
一本
240円

京錦路 井上

個食処

京錦 井上錦

ぐち唐揚
一本
240円

王様コロッケ
一ケ
200円

ぶたひれカツ
くん串
一本
240円

名物
チョコレートコロッケ
100円

CRAB CREAM KOROKKE

These crab croquettes are creamy on the inside and crispy on the outside, a study in contrasts. This ubiquitous treat is especially associated with the port city of Kobe.

For 6 croquettes
Preparation: 20 min
Resting time: 1 hour
Cooking time: 20 min

- ½ cup (120 g) canned or fresh crab meat, drained
- 1 onion
- 2 tablespoons white wine
- 3½ tablespoons butter
- ¾ cup (100 g) flour, plus ⅔ cup (80 g), for the outer coating
- 1⅔ cups (400 ml) milk
- Salt and freshly ground pepper, to taste
- 2 small eggs
- 3 tablespoons panko breadcrumbs
- Sunflower oil

For the Sauce:
- 2 tablespoons ketchup
- 2 tablespoons Worcestershire sauce

Peel and chop the onion. In a saucepan, sauté the onion over medium heat in the butter until it becomes translucent.

Add the drained crab meat, the white wine and ¾ cup (100 g) of the flour. Mix and cook over low heat for about 2 minutes. Pour in half of the milk, stir, then add the other half. Season generously with salt and pepper. Stir again over low heat, then transfer the mixture to a dish. Cover with plastic wrap and refrigerate for at least 1 hour.

Take the mixture out of the refrigerator and divide it into 8 equal portions. Shape each portion into a ball.

Prepare the Sauce by mixing the ketchup and Worcestershire sauce.

In a bowl, whisk the eggs with 2 tablespoons of water. Add the remaining ⅔ cup (80 g) of flour and mix.

Place the panko breadcrumbs on a plate. Coat each ball in the egg mixture, then in the panko.

Heat the oil in a wok, then fry the croquettes for about 5 minutes, until they're golden brown.

Drain them on paper towels. Enjoy with the Sauce.

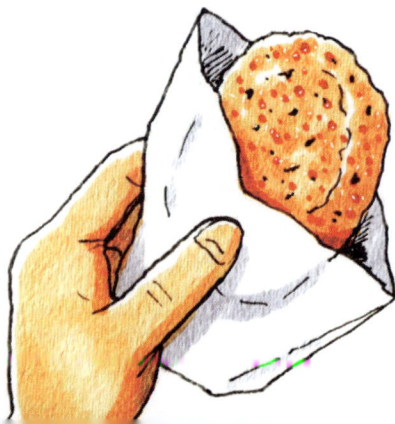

TIP
It's important to refrigerate the crab mixture before shaping it so that it becomes firm and easy to handle. This also helps prevent the croquettes from bursting while cooking.

Tsuyoshi no Croquette Honpo Shop in Nara

This small restaurant won an award for the best cream croquettes from the Japanese Korokke Association. If you don't have the chance to grab one of the five seats available, you can always take these crispy delights to go.

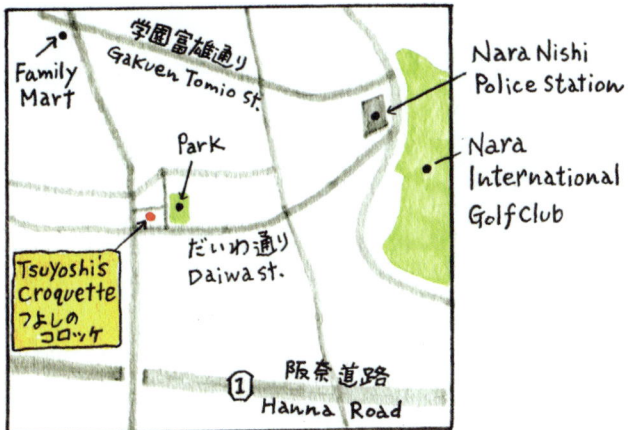

つよしのコロッケ本舗
奈良 Nara
Tsuyoshi no Croquette Honpo

Nara Nishi Police Station

Nara International Golf Club

Family Mart

学園富雄通り
Gakuen Tomio St.

Park

だいわ通り
Daiwa st.

Tsuyoshi's Croquette つよしの コロッケ

阪奈道路
① Hanna Road

Nara, Gakuendaiwacho, 1 Chome-1-1

えびクリーム コロッケ Ebi Cream	¥220	
サーモンクリームコロッケ Salmon Cream	¥190	
肉入りポテトコロッケ Nikuiri Potato	¥180	
ナチュラルポテトコロッケ Natural Potato	¥120	
季節のコロッケ Seasonal Menu	¥190～	

Tsuyoshi's Croquette MENU

DEPACHIKA

Department stores are a true institution in Japan: Isetan, Mitsukoshi, Takashimaya, Daimaru and many more. Major cities host many of these temples to consumerism. Their basements, known as depachika, are entirely dedicated to food and contain real culinary treasures. As you descend the escalators, you discover a vast and lively hall offering the best of Japanese gastronomy as well as all kinds of quick bites and samples to eat.

The word "depachika" is a combination of the English phrase "department store" and the Japanese word "chika," which means "basement." These areas often span one or two entire floors and are directly accessible by subway, with an extensive underground network of shops and restaurants around them, especially in Tokyo.

TASTE EVERYTHING

These luxury food halls offer a full range of Japanese cuisine as well as international dishes. You can even find prestigious French pastry brands. Strolling through the aisles allows you to experience the richness of Japanese cuisine. Since most of the stands offer tasting samples, it's a great opportunity to try all kinds of specialties, from korokke (p. 100) to nikuman (p. 83), not to mention sushi (p. 130).

GREAT DEALS

Right before closing time, there's a frenzy, especially at the seafood section. Sushi and maki are sold at discounted prices. When an employee arrives with 30% or 50% discount stickers, it's the perfect time to buy. You can score a beautiful sushi platter at half price!

A BREAK IN THE PARK

One fun tourist tip is to buy lunch from the depachika in Isetan, the famous department store in Shinjuku, and then enjoy it in Shinjuku Gyoen, the large park right next door. The contrast between the hustle and bustle of Tokyo's busiest business district and the peaceful garden makes the experience even more special!

KATSU SANDO

The katsu sando is a combination of two terms: tonkatsu (p. 110) and sandwich. A breaded meat cutlet placed between two thick slices of Japanese white bread (shokupan) and seasoned with tonkatsu sauce. It's the perfect snack that plays the softness of the bread against the crispiness of the tonkatsu.

For 4 sando
Preparation: 20 min
Rest: 10 min
Cooking: 15 min

- **8 thick slices white bread**
- **4 tonkatsu, about ¼ lb/100 g each (see recipe p. 110)**
- **4 green cabbage leaves, finely sliced**
- **1 tablespoon Dijon mustard**
- **2 tablespoons mayonnaise**
- **3 tablespoons tonkatsu sauce**

Finely slice the cabbage leaves.

In a bowl, mix the mustard and mayonnaise.

Lightly toast the bread and spread 4 slices with the mustard-mayonnaise mixture.

Top with the shredded cabbage.

Spread the remaining 4 slices of bread with tonkatsu sauce.

Also, spread some sauce on one side of each tonkatsu cutlet.

Place the meat, sauce side down, on top of the cabbage. Cover with the bread slices spread with tonkatsu sauce.

Cut the sandwiches in half using a sharp knife. Wrap them in plastic wrap and refrigerate for at least 10 minutes before eating to allow the flavors to blend.

和牛

THE WAGYU SANDO

The katsu sando is usually bought in convenience stores or at train station kiosks. However, some restaurants offer gourmet versions where the pork is replaced with wagyu, the famous Japanese beef known for its marbling, which makes it particularly tender (see p. 32).

TIP
If you want your sandwiches to have an authentic Japanese look, cut off the crusts. You can then use these crusts as breadcrumbs after letting them harden and blending them.

TONKATSU DONBURI

Many cultures and cuisines have their own version of the breaded-and-fried pork cutlet. Tonkatsu is a popular dish that can also be found in bento boxes and sandwiches (see p. 106).

For 4 people
Preparation: 10 min
Cooking: 10 min

- 4 pork shoulder slices, about ⅓ lb/150 g each
- 4 bowls of cooked rice (see p. 123, 4 cups total)
- 2 cups (200 g) thinly shredded green cabbage
- 1 egg
- 4 tablespoons flour
- 8 tablespoons panko breadcrumbs
- 1 green onion, chopped
- Sesame seeds, for serving
- Tonkatsu sauce, for serving (see the Tip for the recipe)
- Vegetable oil, for frying
- Salt and freshly ground pepper

Beat the egg in a shallow dish. Pour the flour and breadcrumbs into two separate dishes. Season the meat with salt and pepper. Dredge the pork slices in flour, then dip them into the beaten egg and finally coat them in breadcrumbs, making sure the coating adheres.

Heat the oil in a wok; it's ready when bubbles appear the tip of a chopstick is dipped in it.

Fry the meat slices in the hot oil for about 5 minutes until they turn a beautiful golden color. Fry in two batches.

Drain them on paper towels.

Thinly slice the cabbage into very fine strips and distribute it into the bowls of hot rice.

Cut the breaded pork into slices and place them on top.

Generously drizzle with tonkatsu sauce. Garnish with chopped green onion and sesame seeds before serving.

TIP
You can make your own quick tonkatsu sauce by mixing 4 tablespoons Worcestershire sauce, 4 tablespoons ketchup, 2 tablespoons oyster sauce and 1 tablespoon sugar until the sugar dissolves.

はも天
Sea eel pike conger tempura
海鰻天婦羅 갯장어튀김 ¥600

撮影OK
Photo OK

えび天
Shrimp tempura
虾天婦羅 새우튀김 1尾(1P) ¥500

Bargain
便宜货 이득
3尾(3P) ¥1,200

撮影OK
Photo OK

アジアツの揚げたて
ご用意いたします!
Fresh fried, please OK.
新鲜油炸好的 갓 튀겨서要

TEMPURA

Tempura derives from a Portuguese dish introduced to Japan by missionaries many centuries ago. These crispy fritters, dipped in a soy sauce and dashi-based broth, have become a staple of Japanese cuisine. Tempura can be enjoyed in many ways: as donburi (served over rice), in a noodle soup (p. 88) and in bento boxes.

For 4 people
Preparation: 25 min
Cooking: 20 min

- **8 extra-large shrimp (about 4 oz/80 g total)**
- **1 onion, cut into ⅓-inch (1-cm) thick rings**
- **½ cup (75 g) tempura flour**
- **½ cup (120 ml) ice-cold water**
- **Vegetable oil, for frying**

For the Tsuyu Sauce:
- **1 small handful of katsuobushi (or ½ teaspoon dashi stock powder)**
- **2 tablespoons soy sauce**
- **2 tablespoons mirin**
- **1 tablespoon sake**
- **⅓ cup (80 ml) water**

Prepare the Tsuyu Sauce:

Place the katsuobushi, soy sauce, mirin, sake and water in a saucepan and heat over medium. As soon as it starts boiling, turn off the heat and let it cool, then strain the sauce.

Peel the prawns, leaving the tail intact, then make a shallow incision along the back and remove the black vein with the tip of a knife.

In a bowl, mix the tempura flour with the ice-cold water.

Dip the prawns and onion rings into the tempura batter, then immediately plunge them into the hot frying oil. Fry, turning them halfway through, until lightly golden, then drain them on paper towels. Cook in batches, a few at a time.

Enjoy the tempura fritters by dipping them in the Tsuyu Sauce.

TIP
Refer to page 98 for all the best tips for successfully frying tempura.

The most commonly used ingredients are shrimp, fish, eggplant, shiitake mushrooms, sweet potatoes, kabocha squash, onions and bell peppers. However, you can switch things up depending on the season: zucchini, broccoli, white mushrooms.

KUSHIKATSU

These breaded skewers, also known as kushikatsu or kushiage, are a specialty of Osaka. Beef, pork, shrimp, vegetables and eggs are just some of the batter-dipped options!

**For 20 skewers
Preparation: 20 min
Cooking: 15 min**

- 4 peeled medium shrimp (about 2 oz/40g total)
- 4 thin slices lotus root or sweet potato
- 2 onion slices
- 12 quail eggs
- 4 eringi mushrooms (or shiitake)
- Panko breadcrumbs (or regular breadcrumbs), for coating
- Vegetable oil, for frying

For the Batter:
- 1 cup (160 g) flour
- ⅞ cup (200 ml) cold water
- 2 eggs

For the Sauce:
- 6 tablespoons Worcestershire sauce
- 1½ tablespoons ketchup
- 1½ tablespoons water

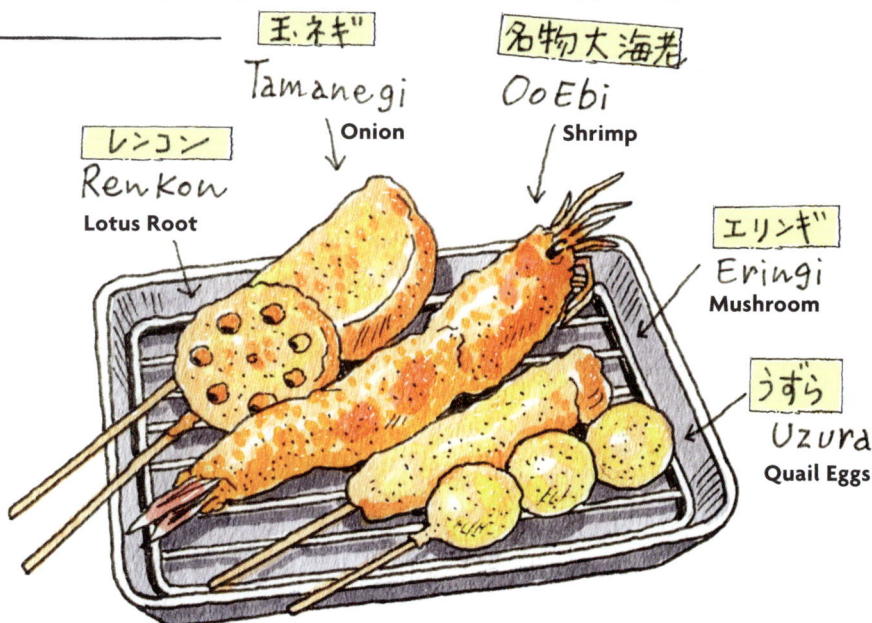

レンコン
Renkon
Lotus Root

玉ネギ
Tamanegi
Onion

名物大海老
OoEbi
Shrimp

エリンギ
Eringi
Mushroom

うずら
Uzura
Quail Eggs

Cut the onion slices in half.

Boil the quail eggs in a saucepan of boiling water for 4 minutes, then cool and peel them.

Prepare the Sauce by mixing all the ingredients together.

Assemble the skewers with the different ingredients (for the quail eggs, place three on each skewer). In a bowl, mix the Batter ingredients. Place the panko breadcrumbs in a shallow dish.

Dip each skewer into the Batter, then generously coat them with panko before immediately plunging them into the hot oil. Fry until lightly golden, then drain on paper towels. Cook in batches.

Enjoy by dipping the kushikatsu into the Sauce.

TIP
You can also enjoy your skewers with a squeeze of lemon juice, shichimi togarashi (a seven-spice blend) or simply a sprinkle of fleur de sel.

かわち屋

Kawachiya Shop in Osaka

〈肉 NIKU〉
- 牛 (Gyu) ————— (1本) ¥120
- 豚 (Buta) ——— (1本) ¥130
- とりもも (Torimomo) -- (1本) ¥120
- ささみ (Sasami) ——— (1本) ¥140
- つくね (Tsukune) ——— (1本) ¥150

〈海鮮 Kaisen〉
- 海老 (Ebi) ——— (1本) ¥280
- 貝柱 (Kaibashira) --- (1本) ¥250
- 白身魚 (Shiromizakana) (1本) ¥170

かわち屋
Kawachiya

タコさん ウインナー
Takosan Wiener
Sculpted sausages

Beer
生ビール

Beer

2度漬け禁止!

Kushikatsu
串カツ

Osaka, Metro
遇天閣
Tsutenkaku

LAWSON

新世界
Shinsekai

かわち屋
Kawachiya

天王寺動物園
Tennoji Zoo

Osaka, Naniwa-ku,
Emisu Higashi 2-chome, 4-15

In kushikatsu restaurants, the sauce is served in large
shared containers. You're only allowed to dip your skewer
once into the communal pot. If you want more sauce, you
can use a cabbage leaf, which is often served as decoration
with your skewers, to scoop up a little extra!

唐揚げ

KARAAGE FRIED CHICKEN NUGGETS

These juicy pieces of chicken thigh, marinated with ginger and then fried, are a staple in izakaya and at street food stalls. If you have any leftovers (which is rare), you can use them to fill a bento for a tasty lunch.

For 4 people
Preparation: 10 min
Marination: 30 min
Cooking: 10 min

- 1 lb (450 g) boneless chicken thighs
- ½ lemon, cut into wedges
- 2 garlic cloves
- 6 tablespoons potato or cornstarch
- 4 tablespoons flour
- 1 tablespoon grated ginger
- 1 tablespoon sake
- 4 tablespoons soy sauce
- Vegetable oil, for frying
- Freshly ground pepper

Cut the chicken into bite-sized cubes. Peel and crush the garlic cloves.

In a bowl, mix the chicken cubes with the garlic, ginger, soy sauce, sake and a little pepper. Let the mixture marinate in the refrigerator for 30 minutes.

In a shallow dish, mix the starch and flour.

Drain the chicken cubes and coat them well in the flour mixture.

Heat the oil in a wok, then fry the chicken cubes for about 5 minutes until they turn a beautiful golden color. Cook them in batches, drain them on paper towels as you go.

Serve hot.

NOTE

For this recipe, it's important to use boneless chicken thighs rather than chicken breast, which tends to be too dry. If you want an extra crispy texture, you can fry the chicken nuggets twice.

TIP
You can replace the chicken with pork shoulder, squid, tofu or kabocha squash.

ONIGIRI RICE BALLS

The Japanese enjoy onigiri at any time of the day. These portable rice packets are mainly sold in konbini (p. 160) and train stations. Most onigiri are triangular, but their shapes can vary—round, cylindrical or even panda-shaped!

①

②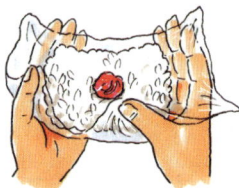

③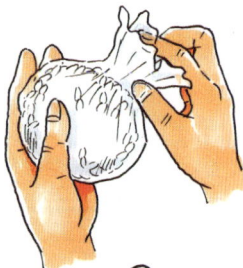

④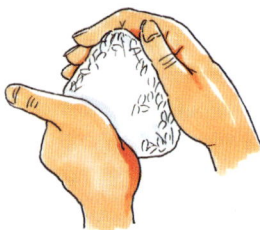

Shaping an Onigiri

1. Spread a portion (about ½ cup/100 g) of cooked rice (see preparation on p. 123) on a sheet of plastic wrap. Lightly salt it and place the filling in the center of the rice (such as an umeboshi, see the next page).
2. Using the plastic wrap, completely enclose the filling with rice.
3. Twist the wrap to form a ball.
4. Loosen the twist and shape the rice ball into a triangle. The trick is to rotate the triangle between your hands to apply even pressure on all three edges, without compressing the rice—it shouldn't be smushed.
5. Once shaped, open the wrap and cover the onigiri with a strip of nori seaweed.
6. Rewrap the onigiri to press it gently so that the nori adheres to the rice.
7. Keep the onigiri wrapped until ready to eat.

⑤

⑥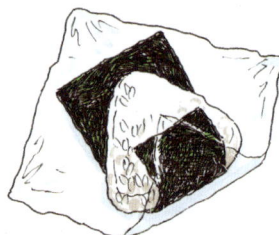

⑦

UMEBOSHI SALTED PLUMS

This variety of salted and dried Japanese plum is a very popular traditional food known in Japan as tsukemono (pickled foods, see p. 166). Its sour-and-salty taste contributes a unique flavor profile. Found in many dishes, often as a rice accompaniment, it also has several health benefits, including aiding digestion. It's one of the most common onigiri fillings.

YAKI ONIGIRI

This grilled version gives onigiri a crispy texture while keeping the rice soft inside. A highly popular snack that I had the chance to enjoy during a break at Okomeya Fumiya, on the path leading to Ginkakuji Temple in Kyoto.

For 4 onigiri
Preparation: 5 min
Cooking: 10 min (in addition to rice)

- 2½ cups (400 g) cooked rice (see recipe opposite)
- 4 tablespoons soy sauce
- 2 tablespoons toasted sesame oil

Place the freshly cooked rice in a bowl while still warm. Add 2 tablespoons of soy sauce and the toasted sesame oil. Mix gently to avoid crushing the rice grains.

Shape 4 onigiri following the instructions on p. 120 (without adding a filling).

Heat up a barbecue or griddle. Remove the plastic wrap, place the onigiri on the grill and cook them 3 minutes on each side.

Using a brush, coat them with soy sauce, flip them over and grill for another 2 minutes. Brush the other side with soy sauce, flip again and continue cooking for 2 more minutes.

TIP
If you don't have a barbecue or griddle, you can also grill your onigiri in a pan or under the oven broiler.

銀閣セット
Ginkaku Set

COOKING THE RICE

Ingredients for 5 cups (750 g) cooked rice
Preparation: 5 min
Cooking: 12 min
Resting: 10 min

- 2½ cups (450 g) uncooked Japanese rice
- 5 cups (1.2 l) water

Rinse the rice in several washes until the water runs clear.

Drain the rice and place it in a heavy-bottomed saucepan. Pour in the water. Cover, bring to a boil, then let it simmer on very low heat for 12 minutes.

Remove the pan from the heat and let it rest, covered, for about 10 minutes.

おにぎり
Onigiri

Shio Onigiri
塩おにぎり
Onigiri variations

Shio Ume Musubi
塩梅むすび
Salt and umeboshi

Sake no Saikyouzuke
鮭の西京漬け
Yuzu and miso

Yuzu Miso
ゆず味噌
Salmon with saikyo sauce

銀閣寺 御米司ふみや
Ginkakuji Okomeya Fumiya

OKome tsukasa Fumiya MAP
御米司ふみや

Kyoto, Sakyo Ward, Ginkakujicho, 65

Jukusei Shoyu no Yakionigiri
熟成しょうゆの
焼きおにぎり
Grilled onigiri

MAKI ZUSHI

Maki are sushi wrapped in sheets of nori. The filling can be endlessly varied, beautifully encased in the center of the rice. The key is mastering the rolling technique. After a few tries, you'll easily be able to do it!

Preparation: 25 minutes

- **4 sheets nori (8 x 7½ in/21 x 19 cm each)**
- **2 bowls seasoned rice (see recipe p. 126, 2 cups total)**
- **¼ cucumber, cut into sticks**
- **¼ takuan, cut into sticks (see p. 165, or replace with tamagoyaki p. 154)**
- **¼ lb (120 g) sashimi-grade tuna, cut in strips**
- **Sesame seeds, to serve**
- **Wasabi, to serve**
- **Soy sauce, to serve**

Place a sheet of nori on the maki rolling mat. Spread a layer of seasoned rice over three-quarters of the sheet.

Arrange the filling in a line on the rice.

While holding the filling in place with your fingers, lift the edge of the mat in front of you and fold it over the filling. Press the mat with your hands to form a cylinder. With one hand, roll the maki gradually while pulling the mat with the other hand.

With each roll, press the maki firmly.

Remove the mat and cut the roll into 10 bite-sized pieces.

Enjoy the maki with sesame seeds, soy sauce and wasabi.

THE 5 GOLDEN RULES FOR MAKING PERFECT MAKI

1. USE A MAKI ROLLING MAT. This is an essential tool for achieving a uniform result.

2. NEVER WET THE SEAWEED SHEET. It will soften with the moisture from the rice and will naturally stick when you apply slight pressure to seal the edge.

3. SPREAD THE SEASONED RICE evenly over the nori. Dip your fingers in water with a little rice vinegar added, to prevent the rice from sticking to your fingers.

4. USE A SHARP KNIFE. The blade must be extremely sharp to avoid crushing the roll when cutting. Make sure to sharpen your knife well!

5. MAKE YOUR MAKI AT THE LAST MOMENT since they don't store well in the fridge—rice tends to harden, and the nori becomes damp and elastic.

INARI ZUSHI

This type of sushi is ideal for making at home. Inari-age, a tofu pouch that encases seasoned rice, is flavored with a sauce that adds a delicate sweetness to these bites. They're often found alongside maki in take-out sushi boxes.

For 15 inari
Preparation: 25 min
Cooking: 12 min
Resting: 10 min

- 15 pieces inari-age (seasoned fried tofu, available in Asian grocery stores)
- 2 tablespoons sesame seeds

For the Seasoned Rice:
- 3 cups (450 g) Japanese rice
- 2½ cups (600 ml) water
- 5 tablespoons rice vinegar
- 3 tablespoons granulated sugar
- 1 teaspoon salt

Prepare the Seasoned Rice:

Cook the rice: Rinse the grains several times until the water runs clear.

Drain the rice and place it in a thick-bottomed saucepan. Add the water, cover, bring to a boil, then cook over very low heat for 12 minutes.

Remove the pan from the heat and let it rest, covered, for about 10 minutes.

Season the rice: In a bowl, mix the vinegar, sugar and salt until the sugar dissolves.

Transfer the hot cooked rice to a large bowl. Pour the vinegar mixture over the rice and mix gently with a rice paddle, fanning the rice to give it a glossy appearance.

Prepare the Inari-age:

Add the sesame seeds and mix gently.

Keep the rice covered with a damp cloth until serving to prevent it from drying out.

Drain the Inari-age tofu pouches and carefully open them (they are very delicate).

Fill each pouch with Seasoned Rice, pressing lightly. Fold the edges to close it and place each Inari-age seam-side down on the serving plate.

TIP
You can make your own inari-age by seasoning fried tofu called abura-age. To do this, follow the instructions from the Kitsune Soba recipe on page 90 (steps 1 to 3).

TSUKIJI MARKET

Although the famous fish market has moved to the outskirts of Tokyo, Tsukiji remains a lively food market just a stone's throw from the upscale Ginza district. While Tsukiji was always known for its fish wholesale market, a large outer market offers all the other food ingredients that Japanese cuisine has to offer. Today, it is the perfect place to sample a variety of freshly prepared, high-quality dishes on the go.

THE AUCTION

For a long time, the early morning tuna auction was Tsukiji's main attraction, but it has now been relocated to Toyosu, 1.75 miles (3 km) to the southeast. This is where the daily auction of tuna from around the world now takes place. Access to the market is now restricted to professionals, but it's possible to register to attend.

TUNA HOT SPOTS

本種 Sushi
Motodane

Tucked away in a small alley off the main market streets, this tiny sushi-ya will delight your taste buds at a modest price, all in an authentic atmosphere.

山長 Tamagoyaki
Tsukiji Yamacho

This shop specializes exclusively in the famous tamagoyaki omelets. Watching them cook them is highly instructive if you want to try making them at home!

築地さのきや Taïyaki
Tsukiji Sanokiya

Taiyaki, the fish-shaped cakes filled with azuki bean paste, take the form of tuna here! Their two specialties are maguroyaki, a crispy version filled with red bean paste, and ottoroyaki, a softer version filled with sweet potato puree.

Kibun Sohoten

紀文総本店 Nerimono
Kibun Sohoten

This store specializes in nerimono, a fish paste used in various Japanese dishes, offering many snacks to try on the spot. You can taste delicious grilled chikuwa skewers or satsuma-age, crispy fried fish cakes (see p. 148).

きつねや Gyudon
Kitsuneya

A true institution in this market: Unlike most stalls here, this spot specializes in gyudon (p. 136) made with slow-simmered beef tripe seasoned with miso. For those who aren't fans of offal, they also serve the classic beef-and-rice version.

Kitsuneya

シュビドゥバ Bar
Shubiduba

This small street bar offers a fantastic selection of sake and natural wines. Try the nomikurabe, a tasting set featuring three different sakes. A few dishes are also available to accompany the drinks. There are no seats here, but the warm atmosphere and friendly service make up for it!

NIGIRI SUSHI

In the land of its invention, there are countless places to enjoy this versatile treat, ranging from Michelin three-star restaurants to pre-packaged sushi sold in supermarkets. There are even conveyor belt sushi chains known as kaiten-sushi.

For 12 pieces
Preparation: 25 minutes
No cooking (except for the rice)

- **1 cup (240 g) seasoned rice (see recipe p. 126)**
- **½ lb (225 g) tuna fillet**
- **Wasabi, to serve**
- **Pickled ginger, to serve**
- **Soy sauce, to serve**

Cut the tuna into thin slices.

With damp hands, take a small amount of seasoned rice, about 1½ tablespoons). Gently press and roll it in your palms to form an oval-shaped rice ball. Repeat until you have 12 rice balls.

Using a finger, place a small amount of wasabi in the center of a tuna slice. Lay the tuna slice over a rice ball. With two fingers, press lightly on the fish so that it adheres to the rice. Repeat with the remaining tuna.

Arrange the sushi on a serving plate.

Enjoy the sushi by dipping them lightly in soy sauce. The pickled ginger is used to cleanse the palate between bites.

Nigiri Sushi Bento
にぎり寿司弁当

DID YOU KNOW?

NIGIRI-ZUSHI

Nigiri-zushi is the best-known type of sushi. If you're making it at home, here's a tip: Shape small rice balls so that the fish completely covers them. Achieving this balance is the key to making great sushi!

TIP
Tuna is the star in sushi platters in Japan. However, you can mix things up by making sushi with salmon, sea bream or even tamago yaki (see p. 154).

DONBURI RICE BOWLS

This is a popular dish consisting of a bowl of rice (donburi means "bowl") topped with various ingredients. Very easy to prepare, donburi preserves the purity of white rice by not mixing it with the toppings. It's a complete meal in a single bowl. Thanks to its variety of toppings, this dish appeals to everyone!

金沢　海鮮丼

Kanazawa Kaisen Don

KATSU-DON: with tonkatsu (p. 110) cooked in a mixture of egg and seasoned dashi.

GYUDON: with beef and onions (p. 136).

TEKKA-DON: with marinated tuna, nori seaweed and wasabi.

SUKIYAKI-DON: with beef, tofu and vegetables simmered in a sweet soy sauce, served with onsen tamago (a soft-boiled egg).

SOBORO-DON: with minced chicken and scrambled eggs.

UNAGI-DON: with unagi (grilled and lacquered eel) drizzled with a sweet-savory sauce and sprinkled with sansho pepper powder.

UNI IKURA-DON: with sea urchin and salmon roe, drizzled with soy sauce and accompanied by strips of nori.

THE MAIN TYPES OF DONBURI

OYAKO-DON: with chicken and egg.

TENDON: with tempura fritters (p. 112) drizzled with tsuyu sauce.

KAISEN-DON: with sashimi of fish and seafood, and salmon roe (p. 139).

築地 どんぶり市場

Tsukiji Donburi Ichiba

This street restaurant, located on the outskirts of the Tsukiji Market, specializes in fish donburi. While they offer classic raw fish donburi (such as maguro tuna, sea urchin and salmon roe), their specialty is a grilled tuna cheek donburi—a true sensory delight!

Tsukiji Donburi Ichiba

SPECIALIZED CHAINS

Yoshinoya is the go-to place for affordably priced gyudon. Their Japanese fast-food concept is popular among folks looking for a quick and affordable meal. They even offer simmered beef bowls for breakfast!

Gyudon
牛丼

Gyudon restaurant Yoshinoya

AMEYOKO

In this large market in Tokyo (see p. 16), numerous street restaurants offer a variety of donburi, mainly featuring fish or seafood. You'll have plenty of choices for a quick meal, eaten standing at a counter.

Restaurant in Ameyoko Market

AUTOMATIC ORDERING MACHINES

Just like in fast-food noodle shops, some donburi restaurants have automatic machines for ordering your bowl. To guide and whet the appetite of customers, photos are often posted. As soon as you purchase a ticket, the order is automatically sent to the kitchen!

Automatic machine for ordering donburi

GYUDON

Some restaurant chains specialize in this affordable treat, which is often eaten quickly for a fast lunch. It's a stick-to-your-ribs treat the Japanese adore.

For 4 people
Preparation: 10 min
Cooking: 10 min (in addition to the rice)

- **4 bowls of cooked hot rice (recipe p. 123, 4 cups total)**
- **¾ lb (325 g) beef, very thinly sliced**
- **4 oz (120 g) firm tofu, drained and cut into rectangles**
- **1 large onion**
- **Pickled ginger (beni shōga), to garnish**

For the Sauce:
- **4 tablespoons soy sauce**
- **4 tablespoons mirin**
- **4 tablespoons sake**
- **4 tablespoons water**
- **3 tablespoons granulated sugar**

PREPARATION:

1. In a pan, combine all the Sauce ingredients and bring to a boil. Add the finely sliced onion, then cover and cook for 5 minutes.

2. Next, add the beef slices and tofu. Continue cooking until most of the liquid has evaporated.

3. Remove the Sauce from the pan and pour it over the hot rice.

4. Divide the mixture into the four rice bowls. Garnish with pickled ginger before serving.

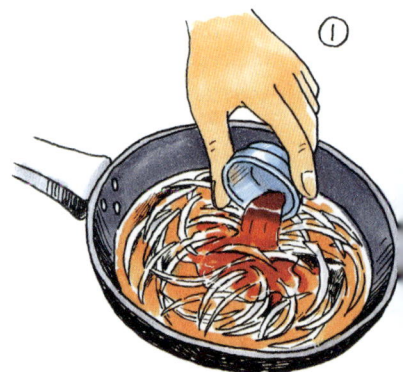

TIP
Prepare this recipe with extra vegetables such as leeks, carrots, green beans or mushrooms. You can even try a vegetarian version, as the sauce is very flavorful.

Tatsuya Gyudon Shop in Shinjuku

Tatsuya Gyudon
たつ屋　牛丼

丼メニュ～ Donburi Menu

- 牛どん Gyudon ¥400
- とりどん Toridon ¥450
- かつどん Katsudon ¥500
- 玉子どん Tamagodon ¥400
- 親子どん Oyakodon ¥450
- かつ牛どん Katsugyudon ¥650
- 大盛り Omori .... + ¥150
- 特盛り Tokumori .... + ¥200

Shinjuku Isetan
新宿伊勢丹

生卵

NamaTamago

Raw egg

Tsukemono

漬物

Marinated vegetables,
see p. 164

新宿駅

たつ屋
Tatsuya

新宿通り
Shinjuku street

Shinjuku
Station

都立新宿高等学
Toritsu Shinjul
High School

Forecast
Shinjuku
South

新宿御苑
Shinjuku Gyoe

新宿高島屋
Shinjuku Takashimaya

Tokyo, Shinjuku-ku, Shinjuku 3-chome,
35-2

Gyudon

牛丼

みそ汁

MisoSoup

Miso soup

KAISENDON

This rice bowl topped with raw fish and seafood is as beautiful as it is delicious, with its appealing contrasts of color. Kaisen means "fresh seafood," referring to the sashimi that garnishes this flavorful and incredibly easy-to-make donburi!

For 4 people
Preparation: 10 minutes
Resting time: 15 minutes
No cooking required (except for the rice)

- 4 bowls hot cooked rice (see recipe p. 123, 4 cups total)
- 1 lbs (600 g) extra-fresh tuna or salmon fillet
- 4 tablespoons salmon roe (or trout roe)
- ¾ oz (20 g) sea urchin
- 4 tablespoons soy sauce
- 2 tablespoons mirin
- 2 tablespoons sake
- 1 tablespoon sesame seeds
- ½ sheet nori, cut into thin strips
- 4 shiso leaves (or 2 tablespoons finely chopped green onions)
- Pickled ginger, to garnish
- Wasabi, to garnish

Prepare the sauce: in a bowl, mix the soy sauce, mirin and sake.

Cut the tuna into thin slices.

Divide the hot cooked rice into the bowls. Sprinkle with sesame seeds and let it cool for 2 minutes before adding the nori strips and tuna slices.

Add the shiso leaves, salmon roe and sea urchin roe. Finish the garnish with pickled ginger and a touch of wasabi.

Drizzle with the sauce just before serving.

KAISENDON OR CHIRASHI?

Have you ever tried chirashi-zushi? This sushi variation's name translates as "scattered sushi." The ingredients are beautifully spread over a bowl of vinegared rice. Kaisendon, on the other hand, is a bowl of plain white rice where the slices of raw fish, seafood or fish roe are arranged more neatly on top.

TIP

Kizami nori is available in Japanese grocery stores, but you can easily make it yourself by cutting a sheet of nori into eight pieces, then finely slicing them together to create the thinnest possible strips.

CHAHAN FRIED RICE

This dish originated in China where it's called chao fan (which means "fried rice"). It's become one of the most popular dishes in Japan because it's often one of the first meals students learn to cook. Simple to make, it's a great way to use up leftovers from the fridge.

For 4 people
Preparation: 10 min
Cooking time: 15 min
    (excluding rice cooking time)

- 3 cups (600 g) cooked rice (see rice cooking p. 123)
- 12 large shrimp, peeled (about 4 oz/225 g total)
- 4 eggs
- 2 green onions
- 1 tablespoon ginger, grated
- 1 tablespoon soy sauce
- 1 tablespoon toasted sesame oil
- 1½ tablespoons sunflower oil
- Salt and freshly ground pepper

Make a small incision along the back of each shrimp and remove the black veins using the tip of a knife.

Cut each shrimp into 3 or 4 pieces, depending on their size. Wash and finely chop the spring onions.

Heat a wok over medium heat. Pour in ½ tablespoon of sunflower oil and coat the wok's surface. Crack the eggs into the wok and, as soon as they begin to set, stir with a spatula to scramble them. Remove immediately onto a plate (they should not be fully cooked).

Pour the remaining sunflower oil into the wok. Set aside half of the green part of the spring onions and sauté the rest with the ginger for 1 minute. Add the shrimp and stir-fry for another 2 minutes. Pour in the soy sauce and sesame oil. Add the cooked rice and mix everything for 2 to 3 minutes. Finally, add the scrambled eggs and the reserved green onions, then season with salt and pepper.

CHAHAN PORTIONS

Chahan is often served in small portions as a side dish to ramen noodles. It's also sold in supermarkets or konbini (p. 160) in the takeout section. During matsuri (p. 48), you can find food stalls where vendors prepare fried rice on a hot teppanyaki grill.

TIP
Feel free to vary the ingredients and add seasonal vegetables and don't forget to look in the fridge for leftovers you can use!

EKIBEN

The word for this taste treat is taken from eki, meaning "train station" and bento, the much loved takeaway meal boxes. You'll find ekiben vendors in most train stations and each region has its own specialty. The most adventurous way to discover these boxed delights would be to take a railway tour of Japan. However, in major stations like Tokyo Station, specialty shops offer bento from all over the country.

Ekiben developed alongside the railway network in the early 20th century and have now become an essential part of train travel. It's almost unthinkable to sit on a shinkansen (high-speed train) without unpacking an ekiben. But these station bento are not just meant to be eaten on trains—many people take them home or to the office to enjoy later.

WHERE TO FIND THEM?

Most ekiben are sold in specialty shops or kiosks located in train stations and even on the platforms. At Tokyo Station, you will find stores specializing in regional ekiben, allowing you to taste specialties from all over Japan without leaving the city!

GREAT SOUVENIRS

It's common to give ekiben as a gift. This makes it possible to bring back a souvenir from a region you visited. To stand out, manufacturers compete with creative designs to offer unique ekiben. The packaging is as carefully designed as the food itself, and it's common to find ekiben with reusable containers.

えび千両ちらし

深川めし

鶏めし

幕之内弁当

鯛めし

牛べん

金目鯛西京焼弁当

牛めし

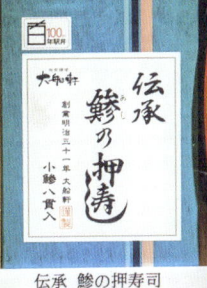
伝承 鯵の押寿司

現在お取り扱いしておりません

会津蔵出弁当

バーベキュー弁当

いかめし

だるま弁当

牛肉どまん中

現在取り扱…

東京弁当

現在お取り扱いしておりません

平泉うにごはん

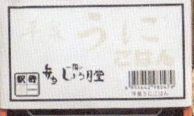

おとな

BENTO

Bento is a true Japanese institution. From a young age, children bring their lovingly prepared meals to school in beautifully compartmentalized boxes. As adults, these meal boxes accompany hungry folksto the office or on picnics.

For 4 bento
Preparation: 30 min
Cooking: 40 min
Resting time: 30 min

- 3¼ cups (640 g) cooked rice (see p. 123)
- 4 umeboshi plums (available in Asian grocery stores)
- 2 tablespoons tsukemono pickles of your choice (p. 164)
- Sesame seeds, to taste

For the Pork Tonkatsu:
- 4 tonkatsu (see p. 110)
- 2 green cabbage leaves, shredded
- 4 tablespoons tonkatsu sauce (see p. 110 for a homemade version)
- 2 lemon slices, cut in half

For the Spaghetti Salad:
- ½ cup (80 g) cooked spaghetti
- 10 thin cucumber slices
- 1 green onion
- A pinch salt
- 1 slice cooked ham
- ½ tablespoon rice vinegar
- 2 tablespoons Kewpie mayonnaise
- Freshly ground pepper

For the Simmered Kabocha:
- ½ cup (120 g) Japanese kabocha
- ⅓ cup (80 ml) dashi broth (see p. 88)
- ½ tablespoon soy sauce
- ½ tablespoon sake
- 1 teaspoon sugar
- A pinch of salt

Prepare the Spaghetti Salad:

In a bowl, combine the cucumber, green onion and salt, then let it sit for 5 minutes. Rinse and squeeze well with your hands to drain the vegetables.

In a salad bowl, mix all the salad ingredients. Let it rest in the refrigerator for at least 30 minutes.

Prepare the Simmered Kabocha:

Remove the seeds from the kabocha and cut it into large cubes, keeping the skin on. Place the kabocha cubes in a small saucepan. Add the remaining ingredients, cover and let simmer over low heat for 20 to 30 minutes, until the kabocha is tender (check with the tip of a knife).

Now, all that's left is to beautifully assemble your bento, starting with the rice.

BENTO

The word "bento" refers to both the container and the meal itself. The container is a compartmentalized box that can sometimes be stacked. Its main feature is portability. There are many varieties, ranging from traditional (lacquered or bamboo) to modern (plastic for easy cleaning).

TIP
- Add pops of color (yellow from omelets, red from cherry tomatoes)
- Carefully cut vegetables at an angle or use cookie cutters
- Use cute food picks for a kawaii effect
- Let the food cool before closing the bento; otherwise, the steam will make everything soggy

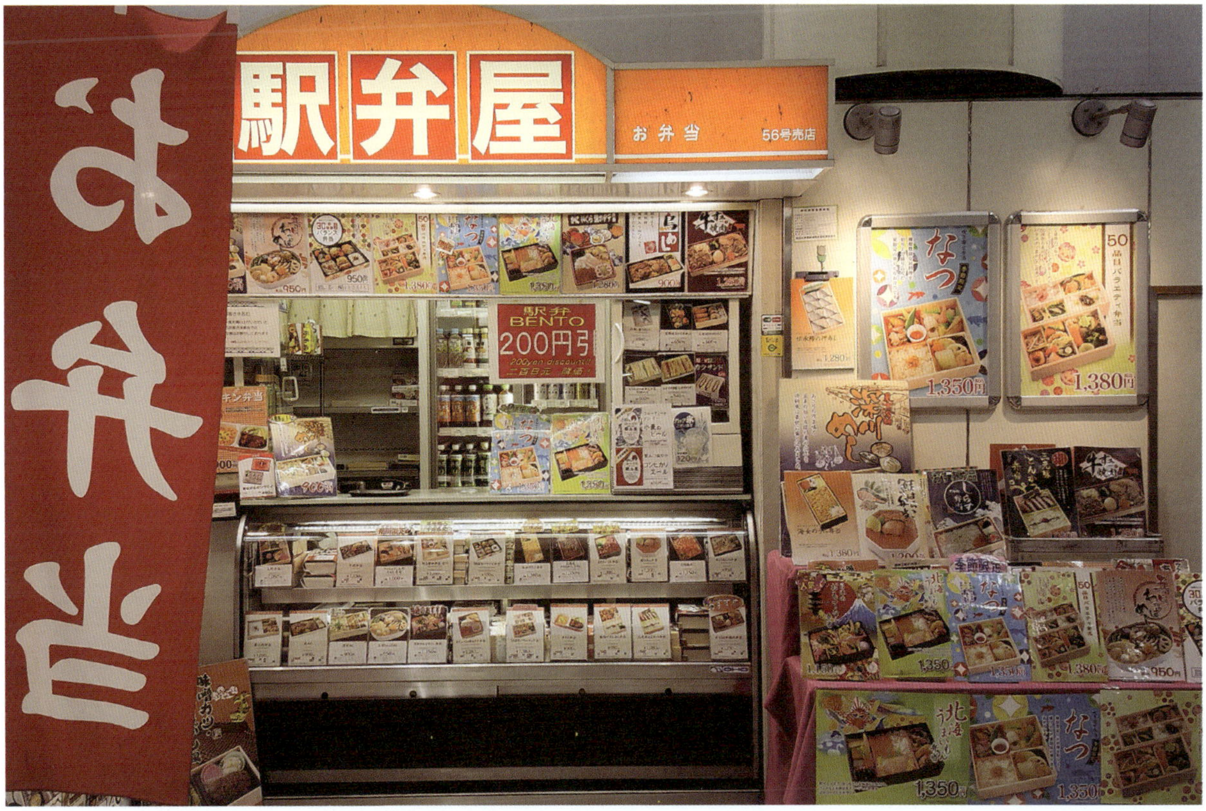
駅弁屋
お弁当
56号売店
お弁当
駅弁
BENTO
200円引
なつ
1,350円
1,380円
950円

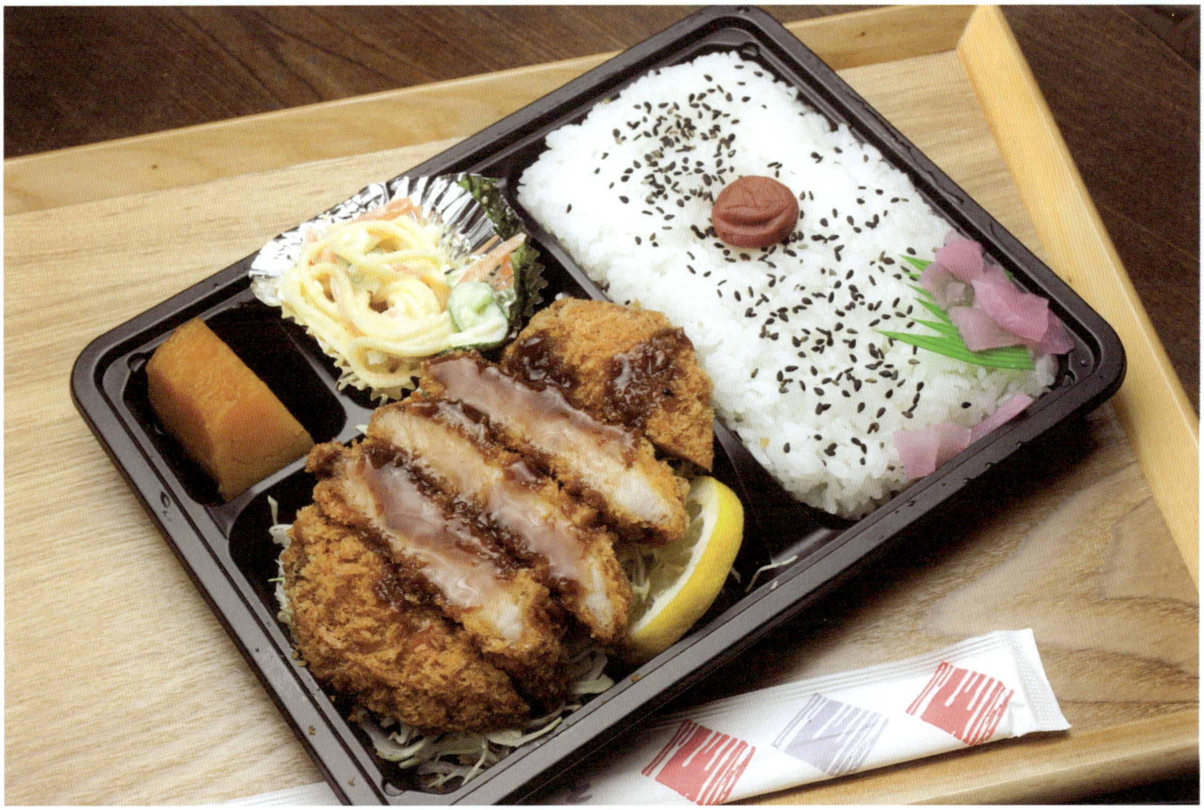

しのび天 258円

エビ天 165円

〇〇〇〇フライ 154円

お好み天 258円

NERIMONO

Often used in simmered dishes, nerimono is a processed food made from seasoned and cooked fish paste. It's prized for its elastic texture, which has the unique ability to absorb the flavors of the broth it simmers in, such as in a savory oden (p. 150).

VARIETIES

There are many varieties of nerimono, and each manufacturer has its own specialties, but here are the most popular ones:

KAMABOKO: A steamed fish paste cake cooked on a cedar board. One of the symbolic ingredients of New Year's celebrations.

CHIKUWA: Grilled fish paste wrapped around a bamboo stick. Chikuwa, which means "bamboo ring," is a specialty of Osaka.

SATSUMA-AGE: A fried fish paste patty. Originally from Kyushu, it comes in many variations: with seaweed and vegetables, stuffed with shrimp or wrapped in a shiso leaf.

HANPEN: A paste made from white fish and yam, steamed. Its extra-soft texture is perfect for absorbing the flavors of seasoning or broth.

NARUTO MAKI: A fish paste roll made from white and pink layers swirled together. It is one of the signature toppings in ramen noodle bowls.

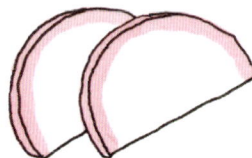

かまぼこ Kamaboko

chikuwa
ちくわ

Satsuma age
さつま揚げ

USAGE

Nerimono is found in various dishes:

ODEN: By far the most characteristic dish featuring these fish cakes (see p. 150).

NOODLE BOWLS (typically ramen or udon) often with naruto or kamaboko.

TEMPURA, mainly using chikuwa.

BENTO, where it can be included to supplement the protein source in these meal boxes.

Hanpen
はんぺん

ナルト Naruto

紀文

Kibun Shop in Tsukiji (Tokyo)

Kibun is a well-known institution where people come to enjoy the famous nerimono, often served on skewers. For a quick bite, try the Tsukiji age, a fried surimi with crab flavor that is incredibly tasty.

總本店

築地揚げ
Tsukiji Age

お好み揚げ
Okonomi Age

ねりもの 紀文
Nerimono KIBUN

チーズちくわの
いそべ揚げ
Cheese Chikuwa no
Isobe Age

紀文

Tsukiji Honganji
築地本願手

中央区立
築地川公園
Tsukijigawa
Park

50

LAWSON

Family
Mart

紀文
KIBUN

304

築地場外
市場
Tsukiji
Jogai
Ichiba

ニチレイ東銀座ビル
Nichirei Higashi
Ginza Bldg.

隅田川 Sumida
River

築地揚げ
Tsukiji Age
1串230円

インカのめざめ
Inca no Mezame
1串200円

チーズちくわの
いそべ揚げ
Cheese Chikuwa 1本500円

まぐろカツ
Maguro Katsu
1枚250円

まぐろボール
Maguro Ball
1本330円

お好み揚げ
Okonomi Age
1本330円

149

ODEN

This simmered treat is comfort food enjoyed as soon as the cold weather arrives in winter. It's served both next to the cash register in convenience stores (p. 160) and in izakayas to accompany a glass of hot sake.

For 4 people
Preparation: 25 min
Cooking: 1 h

- 2 abura-age (fried tofu pouches, see p. 90)
- 2 mochi (glutinous rice cakes)
- ½ daikon, cut into thick slices
- 6 oz (160 g) konnyaku
- ½ lb (220 g) firm tofu, cut into large cubes
- 4 hardboiled eggs
- 4 chikuwa (see p. 148), cut in half
- 4 satsuma-age (see p. 148)
- Karashi mustard (available in Asian grocery stores), to taste

For the Broth:
- 5 cups (1.2 l) dashi broth
- 2 tablespoons sake
- 2 tablespoons mirin
- 6 tablespoons soy sauce

Prepare the fried tofu pouches: Cut the abura-age in half. Dip them in a saucepan of boiling water for a few seconds to remove excess oil.

Then drain the pieces thoroughly in a colander.

Cut the mochi in half. Place a piece inside each pouch. Close the pouch up using toothpicks.

In a pot, pour in all the Broth ingredients.

Add the daikon slices, konnyaku/konjac, tofu cubes and the peeled hard-boiled eggs. Simmer for about 5 minutes over low heat. Add the chikuwa, satsuma-age and the fried tofu pouches. Cover and simmer for 40 minutes.

Place the pot on the table. Each person serves her- or himself according to taste, adding some Broth and a touch of karashi mustard.

からし
KARASHI MUSTARD

This fiery mustard, inseparable from oden, was originally used to prevent potential food poisoning. Today, it's used to enhance the flavors of the various oden ingredients.

TIP
If you can't find fish cakes or mochi locally, you can easily adapt the recipe with other ingredients, such as dumplings or simply potatoes or carrots.

NASU NO SHIRO-AE

Shiro-ae sauce, made from tofu and combined with cooked vegetables, creates a creamy salad that pairs perfectly with white rice. It's often found in bento boxes, where it serves as a complement to richer, more savory fare.

For 4 people
Preparation: 20 min
Resting time: 30 min
Cooking time: 10 min

- 1 small eggplant (about 8 oz/225 g)
- ½ medium carrot
- 4 cups (120 g) spinach
- ⅓ cup (100 ml) dashi broth
- 1 tablespoon soy sauce
- 1 tablespoon mirin

For the Shiro-ae Sauce:
- 6 oz (180 g) silken tofu
- 3 tablespoons sesame seeds
- 1 tablespoon soy sauce
- 1 tablespoon sugar

Wrap the tofu in a paper towel and let it drain between two boards for about 30 minutes.

Cut the eggplant in half lengthwise, then into sticks about 1.25 inches (3 cm) long.

Peel the carrot and cut it into julienne strips.

In a sauté pan, wilt the spinach for 30 seconds in a little boiling water. Remove from heat, then drain well by squeezing with your hands.

In a saucepan, pour in the dashi broth, soy sauce and mirin. Add the eggplant and carrots, then cover and cook over low heat until the liquid has evaporated.

Prepare the Shiro-ae Sauce: In a suribachi (Japanese mortar), grind the sesame seeds. Add the drained tofu, soy sauce and sugar. Mix until you achieve a smooth texture.

In a salad bowl, combine the vegetables with the tofu sauce.

ナスの白和え
Nasu no Shiraae

TIP
The Japanese suribachi, or mortar, has ridges on its walls to effectively grind the sesame seeds. If you don't have one, you can substitute sesame paste.

TAMAGOYAKI OMELET

Tamagoyaki is a Japanese omelet that's cooked in multiple layers. It's commonly found in most bento box fillings, as well as in sushi and maki rolls.

For 4 people
Preparation: 10 min
Cooking: 10 min

- **6 eggs**
- **⅓ cup (100 ml) dashi broth**
- **2 tablespoons mirin**
- **⅓ teaspoon salt**
- **Vegetable oil, for cooking**

In a bowl, beat the eggs with the dashi broth, salt and mirin.

Heat the oil in a pan, then pour in a small amount of beaten egg and cook it into a thin crepe-like layer.

Roll the crepe toward the opposite edge of the pan. Grease the pan again if it's needed, using an oiled paper towel. Pour another small amount of beaten egg, slightly lifting the previously rolled crepe to let some egg flow underneath.

Let it set, then roll the first segment over the new crepe, forming a new cylinder toward the opposite edge of the pan.

Repeat the process until all the beaten egg is used, creating a rectangular or cylindrical omelet, depending on the shape of the pan.

Place the omelet on a sushi mat, wrap the mat around it and press lightly to shape it into a neat rectangle. Cut the omelet into slices.

These Japanese omelets are traditionally cooked in rectangular pans, which help achieve a beautiful block shape. At home, you can make this recipe using a small regular frying pan. The shape will just be different, resulting in an oval omelet.

TIP
Add a tablespoon of sugar to the eggs for an even more flavorful tamagoyaki.

錦魚力名物　はも照焼

福を招く　天然　祝鯛

錦魚力名物　はも照焼

魚力

天然　祝鯛

天然　祝鯖

お土産品・最適品

福を招く　天然　祝鯛

京都名物　はも　天ぷ

弁当　サンドイッチ　お飲物

お弁当　サンドイッチ

駅弁-EKIDEN 開催中！

CURRY PAN

These small buns filled with Japanese curry are soft on the inside and crispy on the outside. Curry pan (or kare pan) has become a popular snack enjoyed throughout the day, sold in bakeries and convenience stores (konbini, p. 160).

For 8 curry pan
Preparation: 30 min
Resting time: 1 h 25
Cooking time: 12 min

- 2½ cups (320 g) curry (see the recipe on p. 92)
- 1⅔ cups (200 g) flour
- 1½ tablespoons butter, at room temperature
- ⅖ cup (100 ml) milk
- 1 tablespoon sugar
- 1 teaspoon dry yeast
- ½ teaspoon salt
- 2 eggs
- Panko breadcrumbs (or regular breadcrumbs), for coating
- Vegetable oil, for frying

カレーパン Curry pan

Start by placing the curry in the refrigerator to harden.

In a bowl, dissolve the sugar and dry yeast in the milk. Let it sit for 5 minutes.

In a large mixing bowl, combine the flour and salt. Add the milk mixture and combine.

Cut the butter into small squares and incorporate it into the dough. Knead for 10 minutes (or 4 minutes with an electric mixer). The dough should be soft but no longer stick to your fingers. Add milk if the dough is too dry or flour if it's too sticky.

Form the dough into a ball and place it in a bowl. Cover with a cloth and let it rest in a warm place for 45 minutes, until it doubles in size.

Once the dough has doubled in size, knead it briefly to remove the air. Shape it into a ball again and divide it into 8 equal portions. Roll each portion into a small ball and place them on a plate. Cover with plastic wrap and let it rest for 15 minutes.

Flour the work surface. Take one dough ball, roll it out into a circle about 4 inches (10 cm) in diameter, and place a generous spoonful of curry in the center. Fold the dough over to seal the filling inside. Repeat with the remaining seven portions. Let the shaped buns rest on a tray under plastic wrap for 20 minutes.

Beat the eggs in a bowl. Place the panko in a shallow dish. Dip each bun into the beaten eggs, then coat with the breadcrumbs.

Heat the oil in a wok, then fry the buns for about 4 minutes, until golden brown.

Drain them on paper towels.

TIP
It's important to use a thick curry that has had time to solidify in the refrigerator. If it's too liquidy, it will be difficult to shape the buns properly. The ideal approach is to prepare the curry the day before—this recipe is perfect for using up leftovers!

KONBINI

These convenience stores, open 24/7, are fully integrated into the Japanese landscape, with more than 60,000 locations—making them a common sight on every street corner!

The word "konbini" is a shortened form of the English term convenience store. These stores offer various services such as cash withdrawals, package pickups, stamp purchases and bill payments. However, they're primarily known for selling food, especially ready-to-eat meals. Over time, they have become an essential part of daily life in Japan.

CONVENIENT!
Onigiri and maki are packaged in a way that keeps the nori seaweed crisp! To open them correctly, follow the numbered steps on the packaging. This allows you to remove the plastic while keeping the seaweed wrapped around the rice ball intact.

MAIN DISHES IN KONBINI

おにぎり
1. ONIGIRI

¥110

弁当
2. BENTO

¥430

サンド
3. SANDWICHES

¥230

あんパン
4. SWEET RED BEAN BUN

¥120

寿司
5. SUSHI

¥890

カップヌードル
6. CUP NOODLES

¥210

コンビニ Convenience store

MAJOR KONBINI CHAINS

7-ELEVEN

Konbini stores first appeared in Japan in the 1970s with 7-Eleven, an American chain that opened the first convenience store in Tokyo. It has since maintained a near monopoly, with around 22,000 stores.

FAMILY MART

The second-largest konbini chain is known for its partnerships with local producers, offering a selection of regional products.

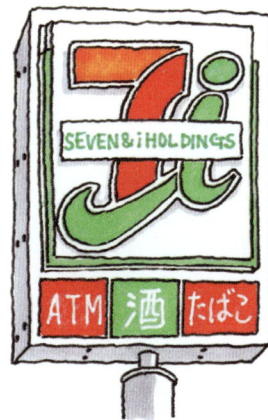

LAWSON

This chain, recognizable by its blue logo, prides itself on offering more spacious stores with a more refined interior design.

団子

DANGO MOCHI BALLS

These small mochi balls served on skewers are a popular sweet or savory treat often enjoyed at festivals. Sometimes, they're tinted green and pink to create beautiful tricolor skewers. Here's a grilled version glazed with a sweet yet savory soy-based sauce: mitarashi dango.

For about 15 balls (5 skewers)
Preparation: 15 min
Cooking: 6 min

- 3⅓ tablespoons rice flour
- 1 cup (110 g) glutinous rice flour
- ⅖ cup (90 ml) hot water

For the Sauce:
- 2 tablespoons soy sauce
- 2 tablespoons mirin
- 2 tablespoons sugar
- 1½ tablespoons potato starch (or cornstarch)
- ½ cup (120 ml) water

In a bowl, combine the two types of flour. Pour in the hot water, mixing until you achieve a soft, pliable consistency. Adjust the amount of water or flour if necessary to get the right texture. Shape the dough into 15 balls.

Bring a pot of water to a boil. Add the balls in batches. Once they float to the surface, cook them for another 2 minutes. Then drain them and thread three balls onto each skewer.

Prepare the Sauce: Combine all the ingredients in a saucepan and heat over low, stirring constantly with a whisk until the mixture thickens. Transfer the sauce to a bowl.

Place the mochi skewers under the broiler (or on a grill) for 2 minutes on each side.

Coat them with the Sauce as soon as they're ready.

TIP
Ideally, grill your dango over a barbecue instead of using the oven. You can also use a blowtorch for browning if you have one.

漬物

TSUKEMONO PICKLES

Tsukemono, which literally means "pickled things," are vegetables preserved in a brine made from vinegar, salt, miso or rice bran. They're ever present in Japanese cuisine, especially in bento boxes and onigiri, where they add an essential touch of flavor, crunch, and color.

Tsukemono
漬物

MAIN TYPES OF TSUKEMONO

The most common technique is shiozuke, where vegetables are salted and pressed under a weight to drain excess moisture. This method often serves as the base for other pickling techniques.

梅干し UMÉBOSHI

This condiment, made from umé, a fruit between a plum and an apricot, is one of the most common tsukemono in Japanese cuisine. The fruit is harvested while still green and pickled with salt and purple shiso leaves, which give it a deep plum color. It is a perfect accompaniment to rice, but beware—its acidic and salty taste can be intense for those unaccustomed to it!

沢庵 TAKUAN

Another classic tsukemono, takuan is daikon radish prepared using the nukazuke method. The daikon is first dried and then pickled for several months in a mixture of rice bran, salt, sugar, and a hint of turmeric (for its yellow color). Some variations include chili for a spicier version!

Nishiki Market Tsukemono

The ideal place to discover tsukemono is in Kyoto, at Nishiki Market (see p. 20). Kyoto pickles are the most renowned, not only for the quality of their locally grown vegetables but also for the expertise behind their preparation.

福神漬け FUKUJINZUKÉ

This mixture of seven vegetables (eggplant, lotus root, daikon, ginger, turnip, etc.) is salted and then marinated in soy sauce, mirin, and sugar. It is the perfect accompaniment to Karé Rice, Japanese curry.

ガリ GARI

Thin slices of ginger are marinated in a mixture of rice vinegar, salt, and sugar. The pale pink hue comes from young ginger, which is naturally rosy. It is the ideal pairing for sushi.

紅生姜 BENI SHOGA

Julienned ginger is marinated in umésu, the residual liquid from uméboshi pickling, giving it its characteristic deep red color.

METHODS	PICKLING INGREDIENTS	COMMONLY USED VEGETABLES
• Shiozuke (salt) • Suzuke (vinegar) • Nukazuke (rice bran) • Misozuke (miso + sake lees) • Kasuzuke (sake lees + mirin + sugar) • Shoyuzuke (soy sauce + mirin)	• Salt (shio) • Vinegar (su) • Rice bran (nuka) • Miso + sake lees • Sake lees (kasu) + mirin + sugar • Soy sauce (shoyu) + mirin	• Umé (uméboshi) • Ginger (gari, beni shoga), shallots (rakkyo) • Daikon (takuan) • Garlic, kabocha squash • Eggplant, burdock root • Various vegetables (fukujinzuke)

164

TAKUAN RECIPE

1 Peel 1 daikon and cut it into pieces. Place it in a container and mix with 1 tablespoon of salt. Let it sit for 2 hours.

2 In a saucepan, bring to a boil ⅔ cup (150 ml) of rice vinegar, ⅔ cup (150 ml) of water, 3 tablespoons (50 g) of sugar and a pinch of turmeric powder (for color) for 2 minutes.

3 Pour the mixture over the daikon. Transfer everything to a jar and refrigerate for 2 days before enjoying.

Takuan

Uchida Store, Nishiki Market

TAMAGO SANDWICH

This egg salad sandwich is one of the has snacks that has spread rapidly throughout Japan with the development of konbini. The preparation couldn't be more basic: a creamy egg salad wrapped in two slices of ultra-soft sandwich bread. But honestly, some of the best egg salad sandwiches in the world are sold in Japanese convenience stores!

MAKES: 4
PREP TIME: 10 min
COOKING TIME: 10 min

- 8 slices of sandwich bread
- 6 large eggs
- 4 tablespoons Kewpie mayonnaise (see Tip)
- Salt, to taste
- Freshly ground pepper, to taste

Bring a pan of water to boil. Carefully drop in the eggs and cook them for 8 minutes. Then drain the eggs and plunge them into cold water to stop the cooking process.

Once cool, peel and cut the hard-boiled eggs into small cubes. Mix them gently with the mayonnaise in a bowl, then season to taste with salt and pepper.

Spread the egg salad on four slices of bread, then cover with the remaining slices.

Let the sandwiches rest for 5 minutes between two planks so that they retain their shape; if necessary, trim the edges to leave only the white part of the bread. Then cut the sandwich in half.

Recent years have seen the emergence of a sweet version of sando. Made with fresh fruit and whipped cream, they're easy to make, tasty and aesthetically pleasing. Their photogenic appeal has made them the star of social networks!

TIP
Kewpie mayonnaise has a particularly addictive flavor. It has a higher proportion of egg yolk than Western mayonnaise and is made with different types of vinegar (rice and cider). It's notably used in the recipe for okonomiyaki (p. 46) or takoyaki (p. 42) and can be found in Asian grocery stores in plastic squeezable bottles.

Katsu sando
カツサンド
(p. 106)

Tamago sando
卵サンド

DORAYAKI PANCAKES

Soft and fluffy, dorayaki is a traditional pastry consisting of two pancakes filled with anko, a sweet azuki bean paste. It is a very popular treat enjoyed at any time of the day.

Makes 8 dorayaki
Cooking: 20 min
Preparation: 10 min

- 1¼ cups (320 g) anko (adzuki bean paste, see p. 182)
- 4 eggs
- ⅓ cup (70 g) granulated sugar
- 1 tablespoon honey
- A pinch salt
- 1 cup (140 g) flour
- 1 teaspoon baking powder
- A drizzle vegetable oil

In a mixing bowl, combine the eggs, sugar, honey and salt. Whisk vigorously for 2 minutes until the mixture becomes foamy.

Sift together the flour and baking powder, then incorporate them into the mixture.

Heat a drizzle of oil in a pan over medium. Pour ½ a ladle of batter into the pan.

Gently spread the batter with the back of the ladle to form a small circle. Cook over medium heat, and once bubbles appear, flip the pancake. Let it cook for about 3 minutes. Set aside under a clean cloth.

Spread some anko paste onto one pancake.

Cover it with a second pancake and press lightly. Repeat until all the pancake batter is used.

Enjoy warm or store wrapped in plastic film.

F.Y.I.

This cake is instantly takes me back to my childhood when I watched the "Doraemon" anime. The blue cat from the future has an obsessive love for dorayaki, and just like my favorite character, I couldn't get enough of them!

うさぎや

Usagiya Shop in Ueno

With nearly a century in service, this small shop is a renowned destination for dorayaki. It's said that this is where the unique two-layered pancake shape was first created. Usagiya also has a tea salon on a nearby street where you can enjoy these Tokyo delicacies.

1 Chome-10-10 Ueno, Taito City, Tokyo 110-0005

チョコバナナ

CHOCOLATE-COVERED BANANAS

At festivals, these chocolate-covered skewered bananas are a must, with stalls vying to creatively present and sell their treats. While the coatings vary between dark, milk and white chocolate, the added decorations make all the difference... and there's something for everyone!

Makes: 4 skewers
Prep time: 15 min
Cooking time: 5 min
Rest time: 30 min

- 4 bananas
- ½ cup (200 g) dark chocolate
- 4 tablespoons sugar-coated vermicelli (optional)

Peel the bananas and prep them onto the skewers.

Melt the chocolate in a double boiler or bain marie. When the chocolate is smooth and shiny, remove it.

Dip the skewers into the melted chocolate. Or use a spoon to scoop out the chocolate and drip it onto the bananas if that's easier.

Before the chocolate coating has hardened, sprinkle it with colored vermicelli. Carefully place the skewers on a tray lined with parchment paper.

Leave the chocolate to set for 30 minutes before serving.

There are many variations on chocolate-covered bananas, such as this white chocolate and matcha coating. You can also sprinkle your chocolate with grated coconut, crushed sandwich cookies or roasted almonds.

TIP
In summer, try putting your bananas in the freezer for a half hour! And in season, try dipping strawberries, which also go well with chocolate.

KAKIGORI SHAVED ICE

This shaved ice dessert, topped with brightly colored syrup, is a summer essential in Japan's hot and humid climate. Many festival stalls and temple-side vendors offer these refreshing treats in a variety of flavors—perfect for cooling down when the summer temperatures climb!

THE ESSENTIAL TOOL: AN ICE SHAVING MACHINE

A must-have for making kakigori, this ice shaving machine creates a texture similar to snow—light and melt-in-your-mouth. In Japan, it's easy to find manual machines where ice cubes are still shaved by hand.

かき氷
Kakigori

FLAVORS

The basic recipe consists of just two ingredients: shaved ice and syrup. However, there are many variations, including the addition of fresh fruits, sweet azuki bean paste (anko, see p. 182), dango (see p. 162), ice cream, or sweetened condensed milk.

The most common flavors are strawberry, melon, watermelon, lemon, and—perhaps surprisingly—Blue Hawaii, a tropical mix of coconut and pineapple flavors.

THE SIGN

To easily identify kakigori vendors, look for the character 氷 (meaning "ice") along with a wave illustration on storefronts or flags.

Himitsudo Shop in Yanaka

All kakigori enthusiasts make it a point to visit this cozy café, where these frozen delights are served year-round. What makes this spot unique is that all their syrups are made from natural fruits.

Beyond visiting this kakigori haven with its wide variety of flavors, I highly recommend strolling through the surrounding neighborhood, which has a nostalgic old Tokyo atmosphere.

Open daily from 8 AM to 7 PM.

MELON PAN

These tasty buns consist of a soft brioche-style interior covered with a thin layer of crisp cookie dough. Their name comes from their melon-like shape—so if you're expecting a melon flavor, you won't find it here!

For 6 Melon Pan
Preparation: 1 hour
Resting time: 3 hours
Baking time: 15 minutes

For the Bread Dough:
- 1 cup (140 g) white flour, plus extra for kneading
- 2 tablespoons granulated sugar
- Scant ⅓ cup (70 ml) milk
- 1 tablespoon butter, at room temperature
- 1 tablespoon beaten egg
- 1 teaspoon dry yeast
- A pinch salt

For the Cookie Topping:
- ⅔ cup (80 g) white flour, plus a little extra for rolling
- ½ beaten egg (25 g), at room temperature
- 3 tablespoons granulated sugar
- 1¾ tablespoons butter, at room temperature
- A pinch baking powder

Start by Preparing the Bread Dough:

In a bowl, mix the flour, sugar, salt and yeast. In a saucepan, warm the milk slightly. Remove from heat and stir in the beaten egg. Gradually pour this mixture into the bowl with the flour, stirring with a spatula.

Transfer the dough to a floured surface. Form it into a ball and knead for 5 minutes. Flatten the dough slightly.

Cut the butter into small cubes and place them on top of the flattened dough. Fold the dough over the butter and knead again. Continue kneading for 10 minutes.

Shape the dough into a ball and place it in a bowl. Cover it with a cloth, then let it rise for 1 hour in a warm, draft-free place.

Next, Prepare the Cookie Topping:

In a bowl, whisk the butter until it's creamy. Gradually add the sugar while continuously whisking until it's fully dissolved.

Add half of the beaten egg, whisking it in, then incorporate the other half. Sift the flour with the baking powder and gradually fold them into the mixture using a spatula until a smooth dough forms. Transfer the dough onto plastic wrap, shape it into a cylinder, then wrap it tightly and refrigerate it for 1 hour.

Shape the Bread Dough into Balls:

Once the dough has doubled in size, transfer it to the work surface and knead it again for 2 minutes to release any air.

Divide the dough into 6 equal portions. Shape each portion into a ball, placing them onto a baking sheet.

Cover the sheet with plastic wrap and let it rest for 15 minutes.

Prepare the Cookie Dough Circles:

Take the cookie dough cylinder out of the refrigerator and remove the plastic wrap. Cut it into six equal portions. Roll each portion out into a circle about 4½ inches (12 cm) in diameter.

Assemble the Melon Pan:

Preheat the oven to 350°F (180°C).

Flatten each bread dough ball slightly with the palm of your hand. Reshape it into a ball and cover it with a cookie dough circle. Wrap the cookie dough around the bread dough ball, leaving the bottom partially uncovered.

Pour some sugar into a small bowl. Holding the melon pan by its uncovered base, gently press the top into the sugar to coat the surface evenly.

Using a knife, score a crisscross pattern on top, then place it on the baking sheet. Repeat the process with the remaining melon pan. Let them rest for 45 minutes.

Bake the melon pan for 15 minutes. Remove to a cooling rack and serve warm.

TIP
For an extra indulgent treat, you can fill your melon pan with whipped cream, strawberries or other delicious toppings!

TAÏYAKI

These fish-shaped cakes filled with anko (sweet red bean paste) are commonly made in street stalls. In Japan, sea bream (tai) is considered a noble fish, traditionally served at celebrations. Inspired by this, pastry chefs transformed Imagawayaki—round cakes made with the same ingredients into taïyaki—cakes with a fish shape.

For 6 to 8 Taïyaki
Preparation: 10 min
Cooking: 25 min

- 1 cup (240 g) sweet red bean paste (anko, see below)
- 1 cup (160 g) flour
- 1 egg
- 2 tablespoons salted butter, melted
- ⅞ cup (200 ml) milk
- 1 tablespoon sugar
- 1 teaspoon baking powder
- Sunflower oil

Mix the flour, baking powder and sugar in a bowl. In another bowl, beat the egg with the melted butter, then add the milk and give it a good whisk. Combine this mixture with the dry ingredients, mixing until you get a smooth batter.

Grease the taïyaki pan, and once hot, pour the batter to fill ⅔ of the mold. Add a heaping tablespoon of anko to the center, then cover it with more batter. Close the pan and cook for 2 to 3 minutes on each side. Then repeat with the remaining ingredients.

ANKO RED BEAN PASTE

Anko serves as the basis for many Japanese pastries. While it's sold in Asian grocery stores, it can also be made at home. There are two types of anko: tsubu-an (chunky with whole bean pieces) and koshi-an (smooth and finely strained). Here is the recipe for tsubu-an.

For 2¼ lbs (1 kg) of anko
Preparation: 20 min
Soaking: 12 h
Cooking: 2 h 10

- 2¼ cups (500 g) dried adzuki beans (available in organic stores or Asian grocery stores)
- 1¾ cups (360 g) granulated sugar

Soak the azuki beans in a large amount of cold water for at least 12 hours.

Drain, rinse and place the beans in a saucepan. Cover them with water and bring them to a boil, then drain again. Return the beans to the saucepan and cover them with at least twice their volume of water. Bring them back to a boil and continue cooking for 1½ to 2 hours, adding more water if needed. The beans are done when they can be easily crushed between your fingers. Drain them and let them cool.

TIP
To make this recipe, you'll need a taïyaki pan, which can be found online or at specialty kitchenware stores.

鯛
き
ち

http://taiankichijitsu.com/

KAWAII !!

Kawaii means "cute" in Japanese. Originating from Japanese pop culture and the influence of manga, the kawaii trend has even made its way into pastries—bringing a sense of whimsy and food fun to both children and adults!

Takeshita Dori

A WALK THROUGH TOKYO'S KAWAII CULTURE

Harajuku is undoubtedly the place to go! On the pedestrian street Takeshita Dori, you'll find plenty of shops where lolitas serve you colorful crêpes or animal-shaped ice creams.

Yanaka Ginza is another great spot to enjoy some kawaii treats. In this shopping alley, the spotlight is on cats. Biscuits, cakes, onigiri—everything takes on a feline shape. Don't miss the adorable cat-tail-shaped donuts at Shippoya bakery!

KAWAII SWEETS

In many stores, and even in supermarkets, you'll find kawaii-themed cookies, candies and cakes. Uchi Café, a brand sold in konbini (see p.160), has even developed supercute wagashi (traditional Japanese sweets) shaped like animals.

KAWAII CAFES & RESTAURANTS

Floresta Nature Doughnuts, Koenji

These animal-shaped donuts are absolutely irresistible. Plus, they're delicious and made with organic ingredients. With multiple stores across Japan, Floresta is committed to environmental sustainability—so you can enjoy these adorable donuts guilt-free!

Shiro Hige's Creamy Puff Factory, Shimokitazawa

Fans of Totoro and Studio Ghibli must stop by this pastry shop and tea salon, where cream puffs take the shape of the beloved animated character. Too cute to eat!

Reissue, Harajuku

For a super-kawaii latte, this is the place to go! The cafe's master barista creates stunning 2D and 3D latte art based on any photo you show him. The results are impressive—almost too beautiful to drink!

JAPANESE CRÊPES

What makes these famous Japanese crêpes special? It's undoubtedly their unique shape. Presented in a kawaii cone form, they're easy to carry and eat on the go. The first shop offering these delightful treats appeared in Harajuku, Tokyo—a district now adored by young J-pop fans.

For 4 crêpes
Preparation: 20 min
Cooking: 20 min

- **1 cup (125 g) flour**
- **1 egg**
- **1 cup (250 ml) milk**
- **2 tablespoons butter, melted**
- **1 tablespoon sugar**
- **A pinch salt**
- **Vegetable oil, for frying**

For the Filling:
- **1 banana**
- **12 strawberries**
- **1.5 oz (40 g) dark baking chocolate**
- **Whipped cream**

Cooking the Crêpes:

In a bowl, mix the flour, sugar and salt. Make a well in the center and then add the egg. Break the yolk with a whisk and begin mixing. Gradually add the milk while stirring, until you get a smooth batter.

Heat a greased crêpe pan (or a large skillet) and spread a small ladle of batter thinly. Cook until the edges are lightly golden. Flip and cook for another minute. Remove from the heat and repeat with the remaining 3 crêpes.

Preparing the Filling:

Peel the banana and cut it into eight pieces. Hull the strawberries and cut them in half.

Melt the chocolate using a double boiler. Once smooth and glossy, remove it from heat, but keep it warm over the water bath.

On ⅙ of the upper portion of the crêpe, pipe whipped cream in a triangular shape, then add ¼ of the fruit. Use a fork to drizzle melted chocolate over the fruit.

Final Assembly in 3 Steps:

1. Fold the crêpe in half, covering the Filling.
2. Fold the right third of the crêpe toward the center.
3. Roll the crêpe to the left, forming a cone.

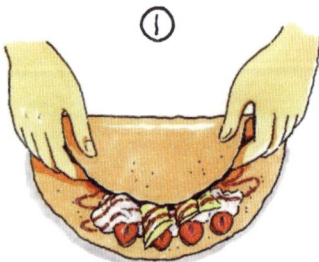

TAKESHITA DORI

This always crowded alley is the heart of anime and kawaii culture. If you love manga and cosplay, this is the place for you. Most of Tokyo's crepe stands are concentrated in this street—an essential stop for any foodie or J-culture enthusiast!

ICHIGO DAIFUKU

These soft, bite-sized treats reveal a beautiful contrast between the vibrant freshness of the strawberry and the delicate white mochi. An irresistibly charming dessert!

For 8 Daifuku
Preparation: 20 min
Cooking: 15 min
Resting: 20 min

- **8 strawberries**
- **⅔ cup (160 g) sweet red bean paste (anko, see p. 182)**

For the Mochi:
- **⅔ cup (100 g) glutinous rice flour**
- **¼ cup (50 g) granulated sugar**
- **⅔ cup (150 ml) water**
- **Potato starch (or cornstarch), for dusting**

Divide the anko into eight portions and shape them into balls. Refrigerate the balls for at least 20 minutes.

Hull the strawberries.

Prepare the Mochi:

In a bowl, mix the glutinous rice flour, sugar and ⅔ cup (150 ml) of water.

Bring water to a boil in a steamer. Place the bowl in the steaming basket, then cover and steam for 15 minutes.

Dust a work surface with starch and transfer the cooked mochi onto it using a silicone spatula. Since the dough is very sticky, be generous with the starch! Divide the dough into eight pieces.

Assemble the Daifuku:

Dust your hands with starch and take one portion of Mochi dough. Flatten it in the palm of your hand. Place an anko ball in the center, cover it with the mochi and seal up the daifuku. Using scissors, make a small incision on the top of the daifuku, then gently open the cut and insert the base of a strawberry.

Repeat the process for the remaining seven daifuku.

TIP
You can make daifuku with a variety of fruits depending on the season—kiwi, melon, mango, persimmon or your personal favorite!

In some ichigo daifuku, the strawberry is hidden inside rather than placed on top—fully enclosed within the anko filling.

188

JAPANESE VENDING MACHINES

There are approximately 2 million beverage vending machines in Japan, meaning you'll find them on almost every street corner. They're an integral part of the Japanese landscape. Whether in train stations, on platforms, in front of restaurants or even in the middle of the countryside, these machines are everywhere and offer great convenience!

WHAT DO PEOPLE DRINK IN JAPAN?

Japanese people primarily drink tea, but they also enjoy sodas and energy drinks with unexpected flavors. As for alcoholic beverages, beer is the most commonly consumed, along with the famous sake (see p. 206), which can also be found in vending machines specifically for adults.

NAVIGATING A VENDING MACHINE

Vending machines are everywhere in Japan, but they often offer unfamiliar drinks. Here's a quick guide to help you understand them:

Water

Energy drinks

Blue labels: Cold drinks

Cold tea

Red labels: Hot drinks

Hot tea and coffee

COMPETITION AMONG VENDING MACHINES

In some areas, multiple vending machines selling the same types of beverages are lined up side by side.

Since each brand operates its own vending machines, they tend to multiply wherever space is available. In high-traffic locations, you might find up to 10 vending machines standing next to each other!

HOW TO BUY A DRINK

1. Insert money (bills or coins) or pay with a Suica card (a transportation card).

2. Select your drink (the buttons light up once money is inserted).

3. Retrieve your drink from the bottom of the machine.

4. Collect your change by turning the dial next to the coin slot, if needed.

UNIQUE VENDING MACHINES

As part of Japan's urban decor, some vending machines stand out with unique themes, artistic designs or seasonal decorations—like cherry blossom motifs in the spring. These creative machines stand out from the crowd!

UNEXPECTED LOCATIONS

Although vending machines are mainly found in urban areas, you can also spot them in rural regions and even in incredibly remote locations—like at the summit of Mount Fuji!

RAMUNE SODAS

A symbol of matsuri (p. 48), Ramune is Japan's signature festival soda. Its refreshing taste makes it especially popular during Japan's hot and humid summers, but much of its success comes from its uniquely designed bottle.

THE CODD BOTTLE

In the late 19th century, a British inventor named Codd developed this special bottle, which uses a glass marble to trap the carbonation inside. The bottle's distinctive narrow-neck design makes it instantly recognizable—even without a label.

HOW TO OPEN A RAMUNE BOTTLE

The fun opening mechanism—where you push down the marble with a plastic stopper—makes Ramune especially exciting for children.

1. Remove the seal covering the top of the bottle.

2. Lift the plastic plunger and detach it from the ring.

3. Firmly press the plunger to drop the glass marble inside, then discard the plunger. Your bottle is now open!

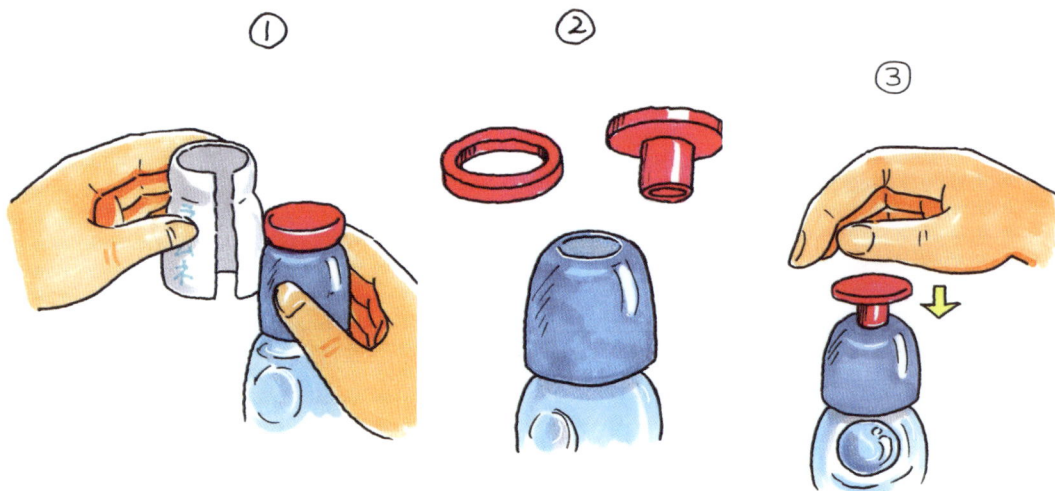

FLAVORS

Ramune is a sweet, carbonated drink with a refreshing citrusy taste, similar to a mix of lemon and lime. Today, it comes in a wide variety of flavors:

CLASSIC FRUITS: strawberry, melon, grape, kiwi, peach and watermelon

EXOTIC FRUITS: lychee, mango, pineapple and coconut

JAPANESE INGREDIENTS: matcha, ume and yuzu

RAMUNE-INSPIRED PRODUCTS

Its unique taste has inspired many products, especially in the candy industry—such as fizzy sweets that lightly tingle as they dissolve on the tongue.

THE BRAND'S SIGNATURE FLAG

Ramune vendors display a flag featuring the brand's signature design elements: bubbles, the logo and, of course, the bottle's iconic shape!

MATCHA MADNESS!

With its vibrant green color, matcha has become a true sensation in street food and on social media. Whether in ice cream, mochi or drinks, it's featured in many delicious treats that can be enjoyed at any time of the day.

MATCHA PRODUCTION

Matcha is produced by covering young tea leaves about a month before harvest. This protects them from the sun, increasing their chlorophyll content while reducing the bitterness typically found in tea.

The leaves are then steamed and dried before being finely ground into powder using a stone mortar.

THE TASTE OF MATCHA

Matcha is a high-quality tea, often made from tencha leaves grown under shade. Premium matcha has a naturally mild flavor with no bitterness, rich aromas and a bright green color.

MATCHA IN KYOTO

Kyoto is the perfect city to explore this tea. In this former imperial capital, matcha is deeply rooted in tea ceremony culture. Additionally, just south of the city lies Uji, a region renowned for producing some of the best matcha in Japan.

INDUSTRIAL MATCHA

While matcha was traditionally consumed as a beverage in tea ceremonies, today it's popular in pastries. Its fine texture makes it easy to incorporate into desserts like cakes, tiramisu, shortbread cookies, ice cream and macarons. Its bright green hue and delicate flavor add a unique touch to contemporary sweets. Many major confectionery brands now offer their products in matcha flavors and colors, making it the new star of modern desserts.

Nana's Green Tea Shop in Kyoto

This is a matcha lover's paradise. The Nana's Green Tea chain has expanded beyond Kyoto, across Japan and even internationally, riding the wave of matcha's global success. Be sure to try one of their specialties: the matcha parfait with mochi balls and sweet azuki beans.

MATCHA LATTE

Just like cafe latte, the matcha version has become a staple on the menus of cafes and tea houses across Japan.

For 1 Cup
Preparation: 5 min
Cooking: 2 min

- **1 teaspoon matcha powder**
- **1½ tablespoons sugar**
- **1 cup (250 ml) hot milk**
- **3 tablespoons hot water**

In a cup, mix the presifted matcha, sugar and hot water.

Add half of the milk and froth it using a milk frother. Froth the remaining milk separately until it forms a nice foam, then pour it over the cup.

If you're feeling artistic, you can try making matcha latte art. This involves pouring the foam to create designs—the easiest being a heart.

Matcha Latte Art in 4 Steps:

1. Follow the instructions from the first paragraph of the recipe above.

2. In a small pitcher with a spout, froth the milk using an electric frother.

3. Tilt your cup and pour the milk in circular motions until it reaches half-full.

4. Once only the milk foam remains, bring the spout close and gently pour in small bursts to create your design.

TIP
To preserve its vibrant color and rich flavor, store your matcha powder in the freezer!

TACHINOMI

Tachinomi is a type of mini izakaya (Japan's version of a tapas bar) where people drink beer or sake while standing and sharing small dishes. Tachi means "standing," and nomi means "drinking." Just like its sit-down counterpart, tachinomi developed as a quick and casual way to grab a drink after work. Today, the concept has evolved into more sophisticated bars that serve high-quality drinks and dishes.

抹茶ハイ

MATCHA HIGHBALL

For 1 glass
- ¼ cup (60 ml) whisky
- ¾ cup (180 ml) tonic
- ¼ teaspoon matcha
- 1 teaspoon lemon juice
- ½ teaspoon honey
- Ice cubes

1. Pour all the ingredients into a shaker.
2. Shake vigorously.
3. Strain into a large glass filled with ice cubes.
4. Top with tonic and stir gently.
5. Enjoy!

Matcha High

酒パチパチ

Sake Pachi Pachi Bar in Nakano (Tokyo)

This standing bar west of Tokyo is the perfect place to experience the lively atmosphere of these local spots, often frequented by residents of this trendy district known for its pop culture. Tucked away in a traditional house in a small alley near the station, this bar offers multiple spaces: on the ground floor, a tachinomi (standing bar) directly facing the kitchen, and upstairs, a more relaxed izakaya-style seating area. The house specialty is motsu-ni, a slow-cooked stew simmered for hours in a rich, flavorful broth.

Pachi pachi is a Japanese onomatopoeia for the sound of applause. Here, people not only applaud the quality of the sake but also the delicious food!

BEER
ビール

Sake Pachi Pachi

Jikon
而今

Yamaneko
山ねこ

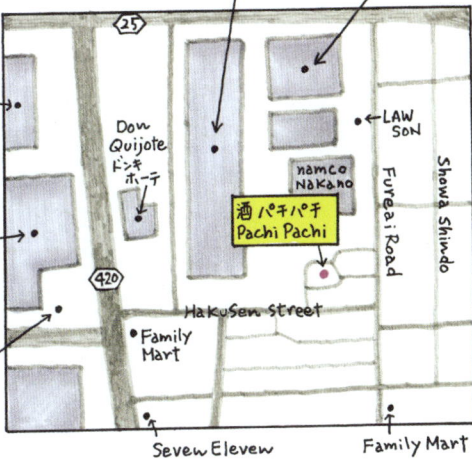

Nakano Broadway
中野ブロードウェイ

NakanoTower

丸井 Marui

Don Quijote
ドンキホーテ

LAW SON

中野 サンクォーレ タワー
Nakano Suncuore Tower

namco Nakano

Showa Shindo

酒 パチパチ
Pachi Pachi

Fureai Road

Hakusen street

Family Mart

Family Mart

Seven Eleven

Family Mart

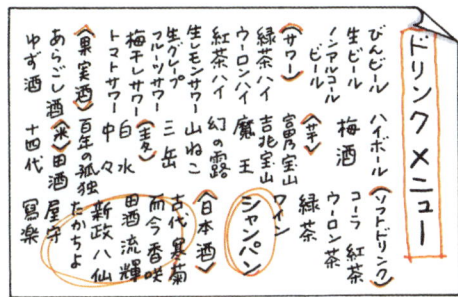

ドリンクメニュー

ハイボール

〈ソフトドリンク〉
コーラ
紅茶
ウーロン茶
緑茶

〈シャンパン〉

〈日本酒〉
古伊勢菊
而今香咲
新政八仙
田酒流輝

〈芋〉
山ねこ
幻の露
魔王
三岳
白
々水

〈サワー〉
緑茶ハイ
ウーロンハイ
紅茶ハイ
生レモンサワー
生グレープ
フルーツサワー
梅干しサワー
トマトサワー
中

〈芋〉
富乃宝山
吉兆宝山

梅酒
ゆず酒
十四代

〈果実酒〉
あらごし梅酒
あらごし桃酒
たかちよ
屋守

百年の孤独
寫楽

びんビール
生ビール
ノンアルコール
　ビール

〈日本酒〉

Tokyo, Nakano, 5 Chome 55–101.

JAPANESE BEER

The nation's most consumed alcoholic beverage, Japanese beer is light and refreshing, making it a popular choice for many occasions.

A BRIEF HISTORY

Beer was first introduced to Japan by the Dutch during the Edo period via their trading post in Nagasaki. However, it was Seibei Nakagawa who, after studying brewing techniques in Germany, opened Japan's first brewery, Sapporo, on the island of Hokkaido in 1876.

Asahi, Kirin, Sapporo and Suntory are the dominant beer brands in Japan. In 1987, Asahi launched its iconic Asahi Super Dry, known for its "crisp dry" taste that pairs well with all dishes. This light and refreshing beer style has since become the standard in Japan. However, in recent years, craft beers (ji-biiru) with more distinctive flavors have started to gain popularity.

SURVIVAL VOCABULARY

BIIRU: Beer
NAMA-BIRU: Draft beer
BIIRU O IPPON KUDASAI: One beer, please.
KANPAI: Cheers!
JI-BIIRU: Regional or craft beer

KANPAI! THE JAPANESE TOAST

In Japan, people toast by saying kanpai, not chin-chin, which would cause laughter among locals—since it's a slang word for "penis"!

WHERE TO SAY KANPAI?

Beer is deeply embedded in Japanese culture, as it's by far the most consumed alcoholic drink. It's common for colleagues to go out for drinks after work, a social practice known as nomikai. The most popular places to enjoy beer include:

IZAKAYA: Japanese-style pubs where small dishes are shared while drinking.

TACHINOMI: Standing bars (p. 202) for a quick drink.

BEER GARDENS: Seasonal rooftop beer terraces that are popular in summer.

YATAI AND FESTIVALS: Street stalls and traditional festivals where beer is always available.

ビアガーデン

BEER GARDENS

During summer, the rooftops of department stores, hotels and restaurants transform into beer gardens, where unlimited food and drinks are often offered. People gather with friends or colleagues to enjoy the cool night air—an essential part of Japanese summers!

THE BIG THREE JAPANESE BREWERIES

ASAHI: The undisputed leader, famous for its Super Dry, a crisp and refreshing beer.

KIRIN: Known for Kirin Ichiban, brewed using only the first pressing of the malt.

SAPPORO: The third major brand, offering a premium beer with a rich malt flavor while remaining refreshing.

SAKE

Sake, also called nihonshu (meaning "Japanese alcohol"), is Japan's iconic drink. It can be described as an intermediate between wine and rice beer, made from the fermentation of rice and water. When no extra alcohol is added, it's referred to as junmai (pure rice sake).

RICE POLISHING

The Japanese are the only ones to polish a grain in order to ferment it; this is one of the specific requirements of sake. The rice intended for sake production is different from table rice. The grains are polished in order to allow the koji-kin to access the shinpaku, the starch core that creates sugar. The polishing rate is always expressed as the percentage of rice that remains.

Rice polished down to 70% (removing 30%) results in a simple junmai, with a deep and structured flavor.

Rice polished down to 60% or 50% (removing 40% or more) produces ginjô or daiginjô, which are more elegant and aromatic.

KOJI

Koji is the key element in the sake fermentation process. It refers to rice that has been saccharified, meaning its starch has been converted into sugar. Without sugar, there's no fermentation and thus no alcohol.

Polished and steamed rice is inoculated with koji-kin, a type of mold (Aspergillus oryzae). The starch and proteins are then transformed into simple sugars. This results in koji-mai (koji rice), which is essential for producing high-quality sake.

THE SAKE BREWING PROCESS

1. The rice is polished.

2. The rice is steamed.

3. Koji is prepared (see above), a process that takes about two days for optimal inoculation.

4. The shubo (sake starter) is made—a kind of yeast mash that promotes yeast growth. It's simply a mix of cooked rice, koji and water. Depending on the technique, this step takes two to six weeks.

5- The moromi (main fermentation) begins. The shubo serves as the base, to which cooked rice, koji and water are added in three stages. Yeast needs about a month to convert all the sugar into alcohol.

6. The moromi is pressed to separate the liquid from the solids. Sake is born!

7. The sake is pasteurized.

8. The sake is bottled.

Steps 7 and 8 may be reversed depending on the kura (breweries).

THE TASTE OF SAKE

Sake is a delicate beverage with an alcohol content between 14% and 17%, only slightly higher than wine. Contrary to popular belief, its flavor profile can be quite complex.

Compared to wine, sake is generally sweeter (with a higher sugar content) and less acidic. However, the diversity of sake comes from various factors: the type and polishing of the rice, the fermentation methods, water quality and the brewer's techniques.

Sake Shops
Sake Pachi Pachi in Nakano (see p. 202)
Shubiduba in Tsukiji (see p. 128)

"BOOKS TO SPAN THE EAST AND WEST"

Tuttle Publishing was founded in 1832 in the small New England town of Rutland, Vermont [USA]. Our core values remain as strong today as they were then—to publish best-in-class books which bring people together one page at a time. In 1948, we established a publishing outpost in Japan—and Tuttle is now a leader in publishing English-language books about the arts, languages and cultures of Asia. The world has become a much smaller place today and Asia's economic and cultural influence has grown. Yet the need for meaningful dialogue and information about this diverse region has never been greater. Over the past seven decades, Tuttle has published thousands of books on subjects ranging from martial arts and paper crafts to language learning and literature—and our talented authors, illustrators, designers and photographers have won many prestigious awards. We welcome you to explore the wealth of information available on Asia at **www.tuttlepublishing.com**.

Published by Tuttle Publishing, an imprint of Periplus Editions (HK) Ltd.

www.tuttlepublishing.com

Yatai: La street food japonaise, originally published by © Mango Editions.

English translation © 2025 Periplus Editions (HK) Ltd.
Photographs: © iStock, © Shutterstock and © Unsplash

ISBN: 978-4-8053-1993-2

Distributed by
North America, Latin America & Europe
Tuttle Publishing
364 Innovation Drive
North Clarendon, VT 05759-9436 U.S.A.
Tel: 1 (802) 773 8930 ; Fax: 1 (802) 773 6993
info@tuttlepublishing.com; www.tuttlepublishing.com

Japan
Tuttle Publishing
Yaekari Building 3rd Floor
5-4-12 Osaki Shinagawa-ku
Tokyo 141-0032
Tel: (81) 3 5437 0171; Fax: (81) 3 5437 0755
sales@tuttle.co.jp; www.tuttle.co.jp

Asia Pacific
Berkeley Books Pte. Ltd.
3 Kallang Sector #04-01
Singapore 349278
Tel: (65) 6741 2178; Fax: (65) 6741 2179
inquiries@periplus.com.sg
www.tuttlepublishing.com

GPSR representative
Matt Parsons
matt.parsons@upi2mbooks.hr
UPI-2M PLUS d.o.o.,
Meduliceva 20, 10000 Zagreb, Croatia

28 27 26 25
10 9 8 7 6 5 4 3 2 1
Printed in China   2507EP

営業中

清酒
白鶴